Palais des Machines

Phaidon Press Ltd
140 Kensington Church Street
London W8 4BN

First published 1994

© 1994 Phaidon Press Limited

ISBN 0 7148 2930 7

A CIP catalogue record for this
book is available from the British
Library.

Printed in Singapore

Palais des Machines
Ferdinand Dutert

Stuart Durant
ARCHITECTURE IN DETAIL

Φ

1 The Eiffel Tower during the final stages of construction, March 1889.

2 Charles-Louis-Ferdinand Dutert, 1845–1906, the architect of the Palais des Machines for the Paris Universal Exhibition, 1889. Engraving after a photograph.

3 Victor Contamin, 1840–1893, Engineer-in-chief of Metal Constructions at the Paris Universal Exhibition, 1889. Contamin was a distinguished teacher and an important theorist. Engraving after a photograph.

The Palais des Machines – the Paris Universal Exhibition of 1889

People were as astounded by Ferdinand Dutert's Palais des Machines as they were by Gustave Eiffel's 'Tower of Three Hundred Metres'. Louis Rousselet, in a popular account of the Universal Exhibition, declared: '…the 1889 Exposition represents … the resounding triumph of iron in modern construction. The Eiffel Tower and the great Gallery of Machines show what degree of perfection the science of the engineer has attained…'.[1]

But the Eiffel Tower was infinitely more visible than the Palais des Machines. Guy de Maupassant used to dine in the restaurant on the first platform of the Eiffel Tower because it was one of the places in Paris where he did not actually have to look at it. Not because of the food.[2]

The Palais des Machines was less flamboyant than the Eiffel Tower and actually had a use. Tancrède Martel described it as: '…the most satisfying creation at the Champ de Mars … It is true that the Eiffel Tower, with its gigantic shafts of metal, the pleasing lightness of its construction … must be judged as a superb work. But …

the Palais des Machines has something more generous in its intentions and a more harmonious grandeur. The Eiffel Tower, despite its nobility, manifests an air of bravado. On the contrary, the Palais des Machines has more modest ambitions, which are more in accord with our present needs. Man here shows himself a victor over matter – rather than struggling against it. He does not vaingloriously attempt to carry his conquests to the skies…'.[3]

Among the most interesting of the many contemporary accounts of the Palais des Machines was that of J.K. Huysmans (1848–1907), the author of *A Rebours* (*Against Nature*) (1884). Huysmans followed in the wake of Victor Hugo in writing about architecture in an imaginative way – his *La Cathédrale*, 1898, used Chartres as a staging post in his own journey of spiritual, Catholic, redemption. Huysmans was fascinated equally by the medievalizing and the modern aspects of the Palais des Machines. He even described the great trusses as shaped like ogees or inverted communion chalices. The Palais des Machines was: 'taller than the highest of cathedral naves … under an endless

sea of glass … when the Edison lamps are lit, the hall appears to expand and become infinite…

Only, as with the Hippodrome and the Bibliothèque Nationale … all the effect is entirely internal … it is ineffective if judged by its exterior… Architecture, therefore, has not actually taken such a new step: lacking a man of genius, iron is still as yet incapable of nurturing an entirely personal production of a single mind, an authentic masterpiece'.[4]

Huysmans was entirely wrong about the lack of a man of genius to exploit iron; the Palais des Machines was, in any case, constructed of steel. Dutert, without a shadow of doubt, was one of the supreme architectural talents of the nineteenth century – the peer of Labrouste, certainly; and, in terms of his actual architectural achievement – major buildings which were to be erected – more than the peer of Viollet-le-Duc.

Charles-Louis-Ferdinand Dutert, 1845–1906

At the very outset it should be stated that Dutert really was the designer of the Palais des Machines. In the past – the past of

2

3

4

4 A view from the Trocadéro of the Universal Exhibition, 1900. Dutert's Palais des Machines was still in place, but it was used on this occasion principally to display food products.

Modernist mythologizing – there have been misunderstandings. Nikolaus Pevsner, in the text of *Pioneers of Modern Design*, which was first published as *Pioneers of the Modern Movement* in 1936, attributes the building to 'Contamin and Dutert'. Significantly, the engineer, Victor Contamin (1840–1893)[5] is placed first. Dutert's role, Pevsner implied, by the act of placing one name before another, was a secondary one – as the mere architect–decorator of what, in the event, was the greatest of all the nineteenth century glass and metal buildings.

The architect P. Morton Shand, also writing in the 1930s, went even further in the diminution of Dutert's part in the design and declared: 'Steel has found its form at last … Contamin's Galerie des Machines was one of the loveliest shapes in which man has enclosed space…'.[6] The triumph had been entirely Contamin's. Dutert was dismissed peremptorily.

Henry-Russell Hitchcock, in his *Architecture: Nineteenth and Twentieth Centuries* (1958) was also dismissive of Dutert's part in the design of the Palais des Machines – he had now become simply an 'associated architect' whose 'contribution was relatively unimportant'.[7]

Before proceeding with an account of Dutert's life, a necessarily brief one, it must be stated that there have been not only misunderstandings over who the designer of the Palais des Machines was, but even confusion over its precise name. It had been called 'the Halle des Machines' and 'the Galerie des Machines', but the incontestable fact is that boldly emblazoned above the street entrance, on the avenue de la Bourdonnais, were the words 'Palais des Machines'.

A summary of Dutert's life is to be found in his obituary notice in *L'Architecte* of 15 June, 1906. It is by Victor Blavette (1850–1933),[8] a near contemporary and fellow École des Beaux Arts prizewinner, who was chosen by Dutert to act as inspector of the Palais des Machines. Blavette seems to write from the position of a close friend.

Ferdinand Dutert was invariably known as 'Dutert the younger' in order that he could be distinguished from his elder brother Arthur – whose academic triumphs at the École des Beaux Arts nurtured, according to Blavette, a fervent competitive spirit in Ferdinand. Arthur had been the recipient of the coveted honour of a scholarship to the French Academy in Rome. Tragically, he was to die in Rome in 1868. He was still very young and his powers as an architect were never to be brought to any real practical test.

Ferdinand Dutert was born in Douai which is quite close to the Belgian frontier. (It was once Flemish and the nearest large town is Lille.) It had been important in medieval times, but in the middle of the nineteenth century it had lapsed into a comfortable provincial obscurity. Dutert began his education in his home town. He was admitted to the École des Beaux Arts in Paris in 1863 at the age of 18. The École's system of architectural education was tightly regulated. Strong echoes of its practices are still to be found in contemporary architectural education. Architecture was not taught at the École itself. Students learned in a private atelier. The École acted primarily as a validating authority. It dictated a student's progression from one stage to the next. It was rigorous in enforcing the highest standards of draughtsmanship. It demanded a thorough knowledge of the latest methods of construction and it insisted upon an impeccable knowledge of the Orders and of Classical iconography.

Students learned the art of architecture, for the most part, by designing projects of increasing difficulty and complexity – which, *gradus ad Parnassum*, culminated in grandiose and, to our eyes, often fantastic schemes. The educational process at the École des Beaux Arts was intimidating to all but the most intrepid students. The École decided exactly what a student should know.

To enter the École the student had first to be taken on in an atelier. All were run by graduates of the École. Some were very good indeed, most were reasonable and the atelier master would prepare his students for the difficult entrance examination.

John Mead Howells, writing in *The Architectural Record* of January 1901, although a student at the École des Beaux-Arts some 20 or so years later than Dutert, described an atelier much as it would have been in Dutert's day. (Howells, who was

born in 1868, was the joint-winner, with Raymond Hood, of the *Chicago Tribune Tower Competition* of 1922.) An École des Beaux Arts atelier, according to Howells, was 'a working association of students, got together to do school work, and criticized and directed by an architect of high standing invited to the position of patron by the students, except in the case of the "schools" ateliers, where he is nominated by the administration of the school'.

Howells spoke of the laws 'written and unwritten' of the individual ateliers. He spoke also of their 'open and concealed prejudices', their systems of rewards and fines and 'worst of all, the co-existence of the two castes, *Ancien* and *Nouveau*, with their shades of interior grades'. A student was merely an 'unregarded nobody' until he had attained the status of an *ancien* – a process which often took two years. Beaux Arts education, by its very arduousness, prepared students for the rigours of the profession itself.

Dutert joined the long-established atelier of Hippolyte Lebas, who had been succeeded by Paul-René-Leon Ginain. Henri Labrouste had been trained by

Lebas – evidence of the restrained progressiveness fostered by the atelier. Dutert was to be among the most successful of all his students – and of the École itself.

A summary of the characteristics of the École des Beaux-Arts system may help us to arrive at an understanding of the complex and sophisticated nature of Dutert's *oeuvre*. The École had its origins in the era of the Enlightenment. It set great store upon the generation of theory – theory which would regulate practice. It sought to devise principles which were universally applicable. It was concerned with the problems of pedagogy. It was meritocratic rather than élitist and it encouraged an extreme form of competition among its students.

While the École always deferred to the Classical past in aesthetic matters, its authorities were far from being unimpressed by the feats of medieval builders. In this respect, Viollet-le-Duc's championship of a rational Gothic in his *Entretiens* was undoubtedly influential.[9] Nevertheless, his association with the École des Beaux-Arts had not, by any manner of

5 E.E. Viollet-le-Duc, Cast-iron supports for stone and brick vaulting, c.1864. At this time Viollet-le-Duc's understanding of contemporary structural principles was limited. Viollet-le-Duc's theories, though not his practice, influenced Dutert.

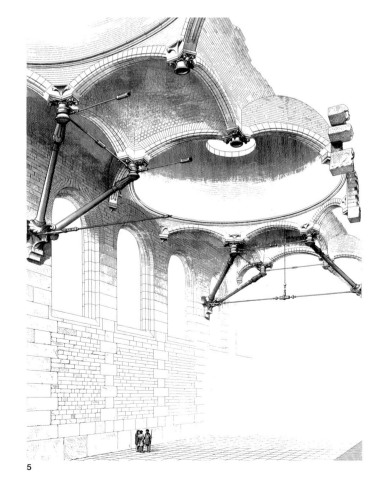

5

6

6 Ferdinand Dutert, Entrance to the Residence of the Ambassador of France in a great foreign Capital. This was designed when Dutert was 24 and a student at the École des Beaux-Arts. His designs for the project won him the coveted Prix de Rome.
7 A commemorative medal struck in honour of Ferdinand Dutert for his design of the Palais des Machines, 1889. Designed by Jules-Clément Chaplain.

means, been a successful one. He left the École in 1864, in high dudgeon, after little more than a year, and having failed to make the impact which was expected of him.

Dutert passed through the various stages of École des Beaux-Arts education with distinction. His first great success was to come when he carried off the Prix de Rome in 1869 for the design of the residence of the French ambassador in a great foreign capital. According to the competition rules the building was not to be designed in any particular national style although, stylistically, one may detect the influence of François Mansart – who in the seventeenth century was the greatest master of classicism in France.

Even without the benefit of hindsight, it would be possible to say that Dutert's scheme demonstrated a phenomenal degree of proficiency. His use of ornament was profuse, though far from intemperate, and designed with particular sensibility. Fine ornament was always a hallmark of Dutert's architecture.

Dutert duly departed from his sojourn in Rome to begin work on the elaborate drawings of the antique – always antiquity

restored to perfection – which were demanded of Prix de Rome winners. His restoration drawings of the Roman Forum attracted the most favourable comments, and these gained him a Gold Medal at the Salon of 1875. He was just 30 and had now shown promise of becoming one of the most brilliant architects of his generation.

Another considerable success came for Dutert in 1875. He was awarded the Prix Duc by the Académie des Beaux-Arts for a project for an Academy of Commerce. The competition for this important prize had been initiated by Louis Duc (1802–79), himself a brilliant student of the École des Beaux-Arts and the most renowned French exponent of classicism of his era.

Blavette noted that Dutert's design for the Academy of Commerce was one of the first occasions on which he put his personal stamp upon a design. Here he demonstrated that the laws of antiquity need not be slavishly, or unthinkingly, followed. In this, Dutert followed in the tradition of Henri Labrouste (1801–75), whose Bibliothèque Ste-Geneviève, of 1836–50, took pragmatic classicism further even than J.N.L. Durand (1760–1834) had

in his didactic publications. Here Labrouste combined modernity – in the form of clearly expressed iron columns and an iron roof structure – with chaste Neo-Grec decorative detailing.[10]

Among the first official posts which Dutert was asked to take on after his return from Rome was that of Inspector of Works for the rebuilding of the Hôtel de Ville in Paris. This did not prevent him from taking part in several major architectural competitions. He came third in the competition for the reconstruction of the Hôtel de Ville at Rodez and was similarly placed with a design for the Faculty of Medicine at Bordeaux.

Dutert's developing skills as an administrator made him sought after in official circles. In 1879, now 34, he was appointed Inspector of the Teaching of Design in the Écoles Spéciales d'Art. In 1881, during the short existence of the Ministry of the Arts, he acted as Director of Education. For a brief time Dutert bore the exalted title of Inspector General of the Teaching of Design. All who came into contact with him in these official posts, recorded Blavette, were impressed by his

7

8

8 Stages in the constuction of the Eiffel Tower, July 1888 to 12 March 1889.

charm as well as his diplomatic skills in dealing with delicate situations. But the work was arduous and induced great fatigue and tension.

Inexorably, Dutert was becoming part of the establishment of the confident and successful bourgeois Republic. The memories of the humiliating defeat of the Franco-Prussian War of 1870–71 had now been all but erased. There were to be rich pickings for architects who were politically astute. Dutert understood the mechanisms of architectural preferment in the Third Republic perfectly.

For narrative reasons, and in order to maintain a consistent chronological account of Dutert's life, the Palais des Machines will only be discussed briefly at this point.

On 8 November 1884, the President of France, Jules Grévy (1807–91), set up a Consultative Commission and announced that a Universal Exhibition would be mounted in Paris in 1889: 'A Universal Exhibition of industrial products will be opened in Paris on May 5th, 1889 and will close on the 31st October

following. The products of all nations will be admitted to this exhibition'.[11]

Days before this announcement, Dutert had submitted a preliminary scheme for exhibition buildings in the Invalides and on the Champ de Mars – the site of the great international exhibitions of 1867 and 1878. One can assume that Dutert must have been close to centres of power. What is certain is that the very conception of a giant cathedral of machinery can be attributed to him. The competition jury set up to judge the overall plans for the 1889 Universal Exhibition awarded Dutert one of the three first premiums and conferred upon him the honour of designing one of the most important exhibition structures.

France was anxious to establish her credibility, not only as a bastion of stability, but as a modern industrial nation. She had lost Lorraine, Alsace and the city of Strasbourg to Germany after the débâcle of 1871. All were immensely important in industrial terms. The Palais des Machines was designed expressly to proclaim France's modernity and tell of her industrial strength. The scale of the gesture seemed almost profligate. In a real political sense,

the Palais des Machines was the most significant of all the structures on the Champ de Mars – including the Eiffel Tower. The Palais des Machines brought Dutert considerable fame, as well as a certain degree of notoriety, it must be said. Douai was proud of him and he was splendidly fêted.

But, like the Eiffel Tower, the Palais des Machines was conceived of as a temporary structure. The Eiffel Tower, against all the odds, has survived. The Palais des Machines was demolished in 1909. Its very ephemerality has militated against it being remembered for what it was – one of the noblest buildings of the nineteenth century – and its architect from entering the Valhalla of architecture.

Between 1893 and 1898 Dutert was to work on the Galleries of Anatomy, Paleontology and Anthropology at the Museum of Natural History in Paris. Blavette described Dutert's exteriors as 'somewhat Northern', by which he probably meant austere. 'But no one could criticize their internal planning, or the skilfully organized lighting.' Dutert's work was unmistakeably personal and at the same

9

9 The Paris Universal Exhibition, 1889. Bouvard's Dôme Central can be clearly seen. It is flanked on the left by the Palais des Beaux-Arts and on the right by the Palais des Arts Libéraux, both by Formigé.
10 The interior of Joseph Paxton's Crystal Palace, the Great Exhibition, Hyde Park, 1851. A contemporary photograph, before the installation of the exhibits, showing the transept.
11 Joseph Paxton's Crystal Palace. A contemporary photograph showing the nave.

9

time modern. He showed himself here, yet again, to be 'an artist who was absolutely in control of himself … above all desirous of conforming to modern needs and aspirations'. Dutert combined the qualities of 'an accomplished technician and a discreet and sensitive artist'.

The entrance to the Anthropology Gallery is paradigmatic of Dutert's work, as well as the work of the École des Beaux-Arts as a whole. It is graced with details and ornament – potent semantics – elements of an architectural culture of a sophistication and authority which no other system or institution could have inculcated in its alumni. The works of Dutert, like Labrouste, Charles Garnier[12] and Jean-Camille Formigé,[13] convince us of the essential vitality of the École method at its apogee in the nineteenth century.

The Museum of Natural History was to be Dutert's last major work, although he had also played an important role in the design of the Museum of the School of Industrial Arts at Roubaix in his home province of the Nord.

In 1895, at the age of 50, the first signs of serious illness became manifest, just at the time when Dutert should properly have reaped the rewards of his achievements. As Blavette wrote in *L'Architecture*: 'Destiny did not wish it so … the illness which was to overcome him brought with it a painful and slow agony although his marvellous intellect remained intact.'

Let Blavette speak Dutert's epitaph: 'The architect who at one and the same time understands his own art and who has the capacity to realize his thoughts … writes a page of history of his own country and his own epoch'.

The Paris Universal Exhibition of 1889

1889 commemorates not only the centenary of the Revolution – with the Bastille stormed on 14 July 1789 the death of the *ancien régime* was inevitable – it also represented the eighteenth year of the survival of the Third Republic. This latter anniversary was certainly of no mean significance. The indemnity demanded of the defeated French after the Franco-Prussian War of 1870–71 had been paid off surprisingly swiftly. The monarchists and Bonapartists, though ever a powerful irritant, had not succeeded in undermining the proud young Third Republic.

As the nineteenth century was about to enter its final decade, secularism and scientific materialism, if not entirely triumphant, were advancing inexorably. The Third Republic sought to identify itself with all that was progressive and its agenda inevitably subsumed a desire to Europeanize the world beyond Europe – the Colonial world. It could be claimed that the Universal Exhibition was the most convincing of all the assertions of Western European self-confidence. Such a display would never be possible after 1918.

One of the earliest industrial exhibitions had been mounted in Paris in 1798 – the sixth year of the Republic.[14] The first international exhibition was London's Great Exhibition of the Industry of All Nations of 1851. France's first international exhibition followed four years later in 1855 on a site close to where the Petit Palais now stands. Unlike the Great Exhibition, which was devoted entirely to industrial manufactures and the applied arts, the display of fine arts formed an important part of the Paris Universal Exhibition of 1855. Delacroix and

10

11

Ingres were major participants. Just over five million people attended – rather fewer than those who had come to the 1851 Exhibition. The Palace of Industry, by Max Berthelin (1811–77), with its central hall and adjoining side aisles, which were roofed with elegant semi-circular wrought-iron trusses, (although obviously partly derived from Joseph Paxton's Crystal Palace transept), may be seen as a precursor of Dutert's Palais des Machines.

The Paris Universal Exhibition of 1867 was sited on the Champ de Mars, with access across the Seine by the Pont d'Iéna. This was to be the site of the subsequent Paris Universal Exhibitions. The exhibition building had a curious elliptical plan which consisted of seven concentric galleries. Sixteen 'streets' – the rue d'Afrique, rue de Flandre… – penetrated the building and led to a central garden. There was a Gallery which was devoted to the History of Labour and a Gallery of Machines – in motion. The 1867 Exhibition was innovative and distinctly Parisian in its daring. There were 11 million visitors and (unlike the 1855 exhibition) receipts exceeded expenses by a very respectable amount.

The fact that France felt able to stage a Universal Exhibition in 1878 was remarkable. As Eugène Pierron wrote: 'The announcement (of the coming exhibition) made a great impression upon all Europe. The renewed vitality of our nation was greatly admired – redeeming herself so soon after the appalling disasters which had befallen her – and the fact that she now felt able to invite Europe and the entire world … to an event in which she would be able to present herself – with éclat – among her fellow nations'.[15]

The composition of the Commission of the 1878 exhibition was impressive. It included Victor Hugo, Viollet-le-Duc, Hippolyte Taine, the historian, (who admired England, but who considered the English had an inferior capacity for abstract thought), Jules Simon, who was soon to become Minister of Education and who had been among the keenest critics of the Second Empire, Charles Gounod, the composer, and Louis Pasteur: a remarkable roll-call of progressives.

Viollet-le-Duc chaired a sub-Commission which examined the architectural proposals and planning of the site. The elliptical organization of the 1867 building was rejected as it had taken too long to construct. The main exhibition building, which is sometimes wrongly attributed to Eiffel, was designed by Léopold Amadée Hardy (1829–94) who was a graduate of the École des Beaux-Arts. The building, which was surmounted by a complex central cupola, deserves a more detailed study by historians than it has so far received. In many ways it was more innovative than the majority of the buildings at the 1889 Exhibition and seems to prefigure some of the structures associated with art nouveau. Victor Horta (1861–1947) was studying in Paris in 1878 and must certainly have seen it. Its influence may be detected – in the curvilinearity and exposed ironwork – in some of Horta's Brussels houses of the 1890s and in the Maison du Peuple, 1895.

'The Exhibition of 1878 left a trail of light in its wake', wrote Pierron, 'and a certain deficit – *sic transit gloria mundi!*…'. Although there had been 16 million visitors – five million more than in 1867 – expenses had been excessive. Receipts were only 24 million francs. There was a net loss of nearly 38 million francs.

12 Adolphe Alphand, 1817–91, Director of Works at the Paris Universal Exhibition, 1889. Alphand had done a great deal of work in the Paris of Napoléon III and had also worked on the Paris Exhibition of 1878. Engraving after a photograph.

13 The construction of the Palais des Machines, June 1888. The two contractors – the Fives-Lille Company and Cail – started at the centre. Cail's scaffolding can be seen in the foreground, the Fives-Lille in the background. This view is looking towards the avenue de la Bourdonnais.

12

13

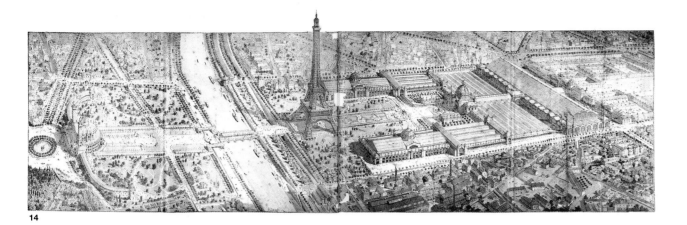

Despite the financial failure of the Exhibition of 1878, as well as a distinctly unfavourable economic climate in 1884, it was decided to stage in 1889 the most ambitious of all the international exhibitions. This took courage – a commodity of which President Grévy, a political survivor, had never been short. The Organizing Committee of the 1889 Exhibition decided that the exhibition was to be financed by the State, and the City of Paris, with the help of the banking house Crédit Foncier de France. An ingenious lottery (which included an entry ticket and ran until 1964) was later devised to drum up additional funds.

Total estimated costs rose to 43 million francs of which the state was to contribute 17 million, the City of Paris 8 million, with Crédit Foncier guaranteeing the remaining sum. Crédit Foncier were to be paid off first, after the closing of the exhibition. In the event, 28 million people attended and there was a healthy profit of 8 million francs to be shared out.

Adolphe Alphand (1817–91)[16] who had done so much to improve and beautify Paris during the Second Empire, was appointed Director General of Works. Charles Garnier, designer of the Paris Opéra – that symbol not only of the cultural aspirations of Napoleon III and his supporters, but also of the transcendence of École des Beaux-Arts ideals – became architectural adviser. Delions was nominated assistant engineer under Alphand and Sedille was put in charge of the fitting out of the interiors of the exhibition buildings.

Mechanical and electrical services were under the control of a Monsieur Vigreux. This was to be an extremely important role and it should be stressed that the Universal Exhibition of 1889 marked the arrival of electricity as an alternative source of motive power to steam – and also as a source of illumination. (It should be pointed out that the 1886 Colonial and Indian Exhibition in Kensington was also electrically lit, although it was very much smaller in scale than the Universal Exhibition of 1889.)[17] The first public exhibition to be electrically lit, albeit a comparatively small scale one, had been held in Paris in 1881 – the Exposition Internationale de l'Electricité.

Paris had an insatiable demand for the very latest in technology.

'The labourers were recruited, foundations dug and the site made ready; in workshops, men began to hammer and fashion those colossal iron structures which were soon to become the objects of our admiration', wrote Pierron. The immense, almost Herculean, task of putting up the exhibition was to be accomplished almost easefully – evidence of the astonishing powers of France for self-regeneration. And, not less, of the enduring vitality of Paris.

The Universal Exhibition of 1889, far more than the Paris Exhibition of 1900, marked a turning point in our collective history. The prognostications of Jules Verne and H.G. Wells, and our subsequent obsession with the technological millenium, have their roots in 1889. For it was in 1889, not 1900, that so many elements in the agenda for our own century – cultural, technical and architectural – were adumbrated.

Besides the Palais des Machines and the Eiffel Tower, there were other major structures on the Champ de Mars. The

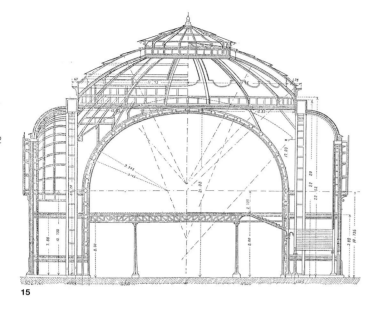

15

Eiffel Tower served as the centre-piece of the 1889 Universal Exhibition while its huge arched base formed a kind of ceremonial entrance, after one had crossed the Seine by the Pont d'Iéna. Closing the vista and directly facing the visitor on entering the exhibition, and framed by the arch of the Eiffel Tower, was the huge Dôme Central of Joseph Bouvard. It surmounted the sections devoted to jewellery, perfume, furniture, textiles, heating equipment and so on. These led to the main entrance foyer of the Palais des Machines. Although one may admire the Dôme Central retrospectively – for its *belle époque* opulence – it failed to represent the new era which the Universal Exhibition of 1889 was ushering in.

Immediately to the left was the large Palais des Beaux-Arts – with its display of French and foreign paintings (Britain was surprisingly well represented) and sculpture. In the further part of the building were the British and Colonial and the Belgian sections. To the right was the Palais des Arts Libéraux which housed anthropology, geography, precision instruments, medicine and surgery.

Jean-Camille Formigé was the designer of these very large pavilions; both had iron skeletons clad in plaster ornament of the characteristic Beaux-Arts kind. Admirable though Formigé's 1889 work was, it lacked something of the startling intellectual clarity of Dutert's design for the Palais des Machines.

So large was the 1889 Universal Exhibition (it was to cover 95 hectares) that it had to be accommodated on two sites. The main site, the Champ de Mars, which was where the Palais des Machines was situated, was of 74 hectares. The Champ de Mars was principally devoted to the products of European industry and the fine and applied arts. There were also some small and, indeed, some not-so-small detached pavilions – Argentina, Brazil, Mexico, Finland, Eiffel's own little pavilion, the Suez Canal Company, Garnier's History of Human Habitation, Gas, the Telephone etc. Bordering the Seine there was a pavilion devoted to electric elevators and another to shipping and life-saving at sea. Pavilions along the Seine – Foodstuffs, Wine-Growing, the United States, the British Colonies – lined the narrow-gauge

railway route, with its toy-like locomotives, to the second exhibition site at the Esplanade des Invalides. Notices, in a hundred languages (including Sanskrit and Latin), warned travellers of the dangers of putting their heads or arms out of the carriages.

The Esplanade des Invalides site has particularly attracted the attention of recent historians, because it was here that the main colonial displays were located. The gardens had originally been laid out by Robert de Cotte between 1704 and 1720. But now an entirely different atmosphere prevailed. France, it will be remembered, was trying to establish herself as a colonial power. It is true that Jules Ferry, Prime Minister between 1880 and 1881 and 1883 and 1885, had suffered a considerable set-back over his adventures in Tonkin, which Clemenceau from the left had exploited. But, in general, the French had been persuaded that colonies would provide ideal ready-made markets for their goods. Colonies would also give France the prestige she so desperately sought.

The Champ de Mars, with its Algerian and Tunisian pavilions, its plaster

15 The structure of Dutert's Grand Vestibule at the Paris Universal Exhibition, 1889. This served as the principal entrance to the Palais des Machines. It was on the same axis as the Eiffel Tower and the Dôme Central.
16 Joseph Bouvard's Dôme Central at the Paris Universal Exhibition, 1889.

16

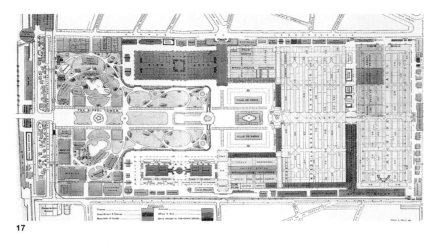

17

17 The plan of the Champ de Mars site, Paris Universal Exhibition, 1889. The Eiffel Tower is on the left; the Palais des Machines is on the right.
18 Jean-Camille Formigé's Palais des Arts Libéraux during construction. Like the Palais des Machines, this also employs hinged trusses. This is probably due to the influence of Victor Contamin, 1840–93, Engineer-in-Chief of Metal Constructions at the 1889 exhibition. Engraving after a photograph.

reproduction of one of the towers of Angkor, Tokinese village, its Tuaregs, Kabyles and Tahitians, must not, for all its fascination, detain us further. But let it suffice to say that it was here that Douanier Rousseau encountered the world beyond Europe. And it was here, in the Javanese village – set up to publicize the benevolence of Dutch colonialism – that Debussy heard the delectable pentatonic scales of the Sultan of Solo's gamelan orchestra. The consequences for Western music we know. Nineteenth century orientalism, now derided, had profound resonances.

The 1889 Universal Exhibition celebrated the triumphs of technology and colonialism. No other large nineteenth century exhibition evinced such optimism. The Eiffel Tower's powerful electric beacon could be seen in villages many miles from Paris. The electrically illuminated jets of the fountains in front of Bouvard's Dôme Central changed colour in time to the music of a brass band. With the aid of two receivers, opera performances could be heard stereophonically – transmitted by telephone from a distant opera house. A powered aerodynamic dirigible balloon

circled above the Bois de Boulogne. Every exhibition pavilion was outlined with a myriad of electric lights. The several electricity generating stations in the Champ de Mars could be studied by visitors and indeed became popular ports of call. Wyndham Lewis's ill-considered remark made in 1914 – in *BLAST* – that the modern world was an entirely Anglo Saxon construct has a distinctly hollow ring to it. The Universal Exhibition of 1889 was the first festival of modernity. Filippo Marinetti's Futurism – founded upon a naively idealistic view of modernity – surely has its roots in the Exhibition of 1889.

But the darker side of the coming twentieth century was also to be made manifest in the Champ de Mars – the very place itself bears the name of the ancient god of war. Industrial advance has always brought new methods of mechanized violence in its wake and prominent displays of heavy artillery by armament manufacturers drew large crowds of visitors.

The Palais des Machines
As we saw earlier, Dutert was one of the first architects to stake a claim in the 1889

exhibition with a provisional scheme for the layout of the Champ de Mars. He was also to be one of the winners of the competition for exhibition structures for which the results were announced in May 1886. Jean-Camille Formigé and the partnership of Gustave Eiffel (1832–1923) and Stephen Sauvestre (b. 1847) were the other winners.[18]

Dutert's initial design for the Palais des Machines took the form which was typical of earlier Parisian exhibition buildings and consisted simply of five side-by-side galleries. The origin of the subsequent idea of a single gallery spanned by immense steel trusses of 110 metres span (rather over 360 feet) is somewhat obscure. However, an important consideration was the very poor state of the site which had been ravaged by the digging of the foundations for the previous exhibition buildings. A structure with large spans would obviously involve less costly site preparation. Contemporaries attribute the origin of the single span solution to Dutert. The logic of this scheme would certainly have been more pleasing to him aesthetically.

18

19 The Palais des Machines under construction in 1888. This shows the semi-prefabricated method of the Fives-Lille Company.
20 A detail of one of the trusses, 1889.

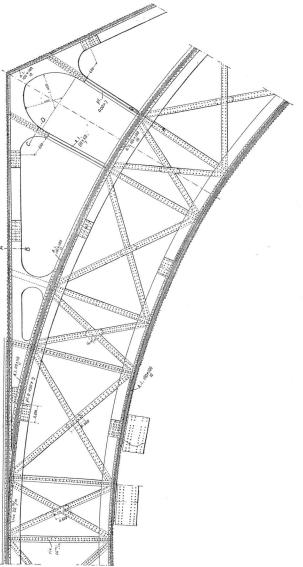

19

20

21

Blavette, in Dutert's obituary notice of 1906, is quite categorical that the idea of the large trusses came from Dutert. Blavette is worth hearing at some length. Dutert's true part in the Palais des Machines project will become apparent: '…from the outset of his researches [Dutert] felt that a structure which was to be destined to accommodate powerful machines … must itself be in sympathy with these machines and be an appropriate expression of their potency. From that point to the conception of the huge gallery, which the whole world was to know, was but a short step away…

'Dutert's proposal, though certainly worthy of consideration, aroused a degree of lively opposition. It scared the mathematicians – who were accomplished in devising the formulae to represent the stresses imposed upon materials. The more moderate schemes which were put forward made those of Dutert seem best put aside, like the pipe-dreams of an artist. But Dutert knew that his dreamed-of building was realizable and that there was no reason whatsoever why the loads of the roof trusses which had already been

constructed in the era could not be surpassed. He sensed correctly. And thanks to the support of M. Lockroy[19] – who had authorized the building of a Tower of Three Hundred Metres and who was not intimidated by an equally daring scheme – Dutert's theories were accepted. Nevertheless, Dutert's project was to be subject to modifications which facilitated and simplified construction and which, to our way of thinking, made it none the less daring.

'The immense gallery which [Dutert] had conceived was intended to terminate with a hipped-roof at each end; these two hipped roofs would have had to neutralize equal and opposing forces and also ensure the stability of the whole structure with cross braces…

'Each of the four corners of this "Temple of Steam" were to be buttressed by three tall chimneys which would accord with the nature of the other exhibition buildings.

'Time was passing and discussions seemed endless … Dutert understood that in view of the fact that the essentials of his composition had been adopted he had the

duty, in the interests of a favourable outcome for the Exhibition, to concede that, after all, his building was to be no more than an appendage. But, with this concession made, he was to become immovable over other matters – everything, from the great skeleton to the tiniest details, had to conform to his drawings. His role must have stopped short only at the mathematical determination of the thickness of the metal employed…'.

Although this is the testimony of a loyal colleague, writing an obituary, it does seem to establish incontrovertibly that Dutert was the designer – in the sense in which we ourselves understand it – of the Palais des Machines. Also, the 1891 portrait of Dutert, by Jean-Joseph Weerts (shown in the centenary exhibition of the 1889 exhibition at the Musée d'Orsay) shows him at his work-table with a drawing pinned to the wall, not of the Palais des Machines, as a work of architecture, but simply of a large-scale detail of one of the great trusses. The truss is presented in the portrait in almost the way it would have been if it were an equation of momentous mathematical significance.

21 An aerial view of Dutert's Palais des Machines, showing an intermediate form of the design. The 'side chapels' are still retained on the street elevations, but the hipped roof has by now been abandoned.
22 An aerial view of the Paris Universal Exhibition, 1889. This shows Dutert's first design for the Palais des Machines, which had a hipped roof.

23 The façade, on the avenue de la Bourdonnais, of the Palais des Machines, during the Paris Universal Exhibition, 1889. J.K. Huysmans, in his account of the building in *Certains* (Paris, 1889) evidently entered it from the aisle which led from the Dôme Central. In consequence he seems to have been unaware that it actually had an exterior elevation. Engraving after a photograph.
24 Jules Grévy (1807–91), the President of France, inspecting the Palais des Machines shortly before its completion. Engraving after a photograph.

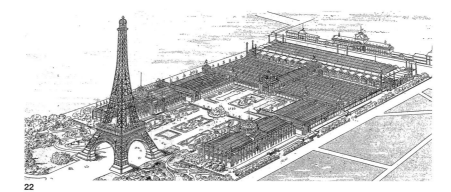

22

23

24

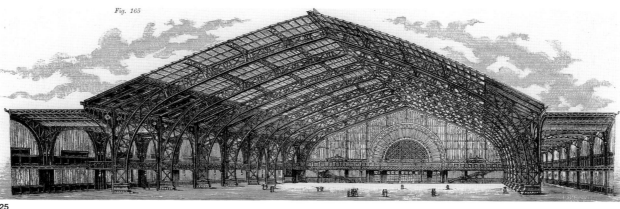

Fig. 165

25

25 A sectional perspective of the Palais des Machines. The bases of the trusses have been treated in a commonplace way and the hinges have been concealed. Presumably, this drawing shows an intermediate stage in the design.

26 The façade of the Palais des Machines on the avenue de la Bourdonnais in its final form. A classical discipline, which derives from Dutert's training at the École des Beaux-Arts, prevails; but it is also possible to detect medievalizing aspects. These derive from the tradition of modernized Gothic initiated by Viollet-le-Duc.

17

What did Blavette mean by his observation that Dutert had had to concede that his building was to be 'no more than an appendage'? This refers, in reality, to the fact that the ideal École des Beaux-Arts project (and Blavette, like Dutert, was a Beaux-Arts man) was conceived of as an entirely autonomous building, in a place of honour, where its façade could be admired. The Palais des Machines was hidden behind Bouvard's Dôme Central.

The principal entrance to the Palais des Machines was through a large vestibule leading off Bouvard's building and situated on the main axis of the exhibition. It was for this reason that Huysmans, while admiring Dutert's interior, did not recognize that the Palais des Machines actually had an exterior. And even a handsome façade on the avenue de la Bourdonnais. He would undoubtedly have approached the Palais des Machines through the 'Grand Vestibule', which was the typical point of entry for the exhibition visitor.

Dutert's earlier design for the Palais des Machines (the one with the hipped roof referred to by Blavette) was flanked by a series of smaller structures, of which there were some 19 longitudinally. There were also seven of these at either end. These smaller, apparently medievalizing, structures correspond – to cite a fairly obvious example – with the side-chapels which were added, somewhat later, to the choir of La-Charité-sur-Loire, Nièvre, which had been consecrated in 1107. There can be little doubt that Dutert's borrowing of a medieval form, which was skilfully transformed into steel, was inspired by the teachings of Viollet-le-Duc. Interestingly, the curved form of the small trusses of the 'side-chapels' is that of a section through a Romanesque cross-vault. In the final scheme the 'side-chapels' were only retained on the longitudinal elevations.

Dutert, as Blavette said, was talked out of the hipped-roofs because of the sheer technical problems they imposed; it is easy enough to imagine the very considerable additional stresses which would be imposed upon the trusses – whatever form they took – at either end of the structure. The engineering problem, though soluble, could not have been resolved with real elegance. Also, the architectural solution was less than satisfactory. The 'side-chapels' which would have constituted the façades of the avenue de la Bourdonnais as well as the avenue de Suffren ends of the Palais des Machines also lacked any dramatic monumentality.

The structural and, in the event, architectural resolution came with the idea of creating double trusses at either end of the Palais des Machines. These were set forward of a curtain wall and left fully exposed. These curtain walls made possible façades with considerable potential for architectural treatment in the grand École des Beaux-Arts manner. But here, at the Champ de Mars, the leitmotiv was to be metal and glass. Dutert was to respond magnificently to a suggestion that came from a source that we may never be able to identify.

The great curtain walls seen from the avenue de la Bourdonnais and avenue de Suffren had to withstand considerable wind-loads and were consequently braced vertically with light lattice-trusses which diminished in depth as they approached the ogee-shaped roof itself. These façades, each different, with their brilliantly-coloured stained glass, their moulded plaster-work

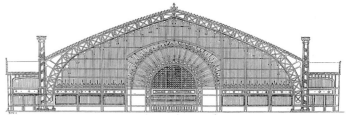

26

27

28

and their patterned brickwork, were articulated in a most dexterous way. These seem almost to accord with Alberti's ideas on the scholarly organization of the various elements of a façade – which he called *partitio*, or 'compartition'.[20]

The curtain walls of the Palais des Machines were certainly the largest of the nineteenth century. It could be argued that they were among the first true curtain walls, although I.K. Brunel and Matthew Digby Wyatt's train shed for the Great Western Railway at Paddington, of 1852-54, was glazed at the far end; so, too, was Leonce Reynaud's Gare d'Austerlitz, Paris, of 1859–62. But, of course, these glazed ends were a good deal smaller than Dutert's façades and cannot really be considered to have been significant components in a prestigious and formal architectural composition. (G. Salard and T. Seyrig's main station for Budapest of 1875–77 had a large curtain wall – Eiffel collaborated in the project which Dutert probably knew.)

As for precursors of the Palais des Machines, there were those listed here – all those selected have some relationship to it, even if remote. For it should be remembered that works of architecture and civil engineering were to become internationally known through publications during the nineteenth century. Although, with the coming of the railways, travel was very easy in Europe, it was, after all, infinitely easier for an architect or an engineer to consult a journal than to visit a novel bridge or building.

Among exhibition buildings there was Joseph Paxton's Great Exhibition Building – Crystal Palace – Hyde Park, London, (1850–51), which was re–erected at Sydenham, in a somewhat enlarged form in 1854, re-employing the original cast and wrought iron components. Spans were unimpressive when compared with those of the Palais des Machines, but the history of the metal and glass exhibition building begins with the Crystal Palace. Pre-1889 French exhibition buildings have already been discussed briefly. It is the railway train shed to which we ought now to turn. For it is this building-type which was the real progenitor of the Palais des Machines.

Victoria Station, London, built between 1860 and 1862 and designed by John Fowler, has elegant curved trusses spanning nearly 40 metres. But a multiplicity of un-architectural tie-bars seem to render this structure unacceptable according to Beaux-Arts aesthetic canons. (William Baker and Francis Stevenson's Lime Street Station, Liverpool, 1867–79, has a span of 61 metres, but this also employs tie-bars.)

W.H. Barlow and R.M. Ordish's train shed for St Pancras Station, 1868 (Sir George Gilbert Scott's contributions fall outside the scope of this monograph) had curved trusses which spanned 74 metres. This was very much admired and was widely publicized – it appeared in the *Encyclopédie d'Architecture*, volume 2, 1873 (plates 94, 98 and 120) of which Viollet-le-Duc was the principal editor. It seems almost inevitable that Dutert would have seen the precise steel engravings of the trusses which appeared there – and drawn inspiration from them.

The St Pancras Station train shed was constructed just over two decades before the Palais des Machines. The advances in structural engineering which had taken place in this interval of time are epitomized by Dutert's work. Interestingly, another

27 A contemporary photograph of the transept of Joseph Paxton's Crystal Palace at the Great Exhibition, 1851. (The arch of the transept incorporated an ingenious electric clock designed by Owen Jones.)

28 A recent photograph of the train shed of St Pancras Station, London, by Barlow and Ordish, 1868.

29 A detail of a truss, St Pancras Station, London, by Barlow and Ordish, 1868. This spans approximately one third less than the trusses of the Palais des Machines. This steel engraving was originally published in the *Encyclopédie d'Architecture*. It is likely that Dutert would have seen this drawing.

30 A detail of a truss at the Palais des Machines, 1889. Although Dutert would have designed the trusses of the building, Victor Contamin, the Engineer-in-Chief of Metal Construction at the 1889 Exhibition, would have been responsible for specifying the thicknesses of steel employed.

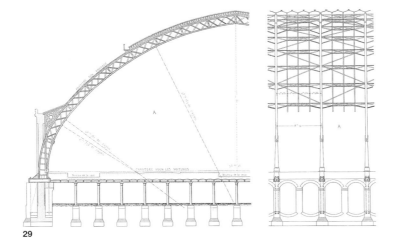

29

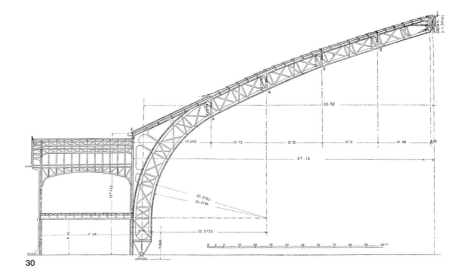

30

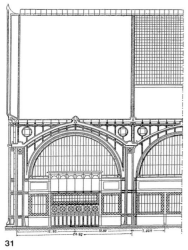

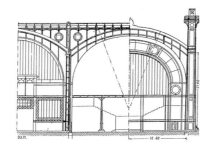

31 Drawings showing the types of subsidiary structures ('side chapels') used in the Palais des Machines, 1889.
32 Part of the side elevation, on the avenue de la Motte Piquet, which crossed the avenue de la Bourdonnais. The photograph was taken shortly before the demolition of the Palais des Machines in 1909.

31

32

406. PARIS — La Galerie des Machines   C. M.

33

34

33 The Palais des Machines shortly before its demolition. It was sometimes used as an indoor cycling track. From a contemporary postcard.
34 The Palais des Machines. From a photograph taken shortly before its demolition in 1909.

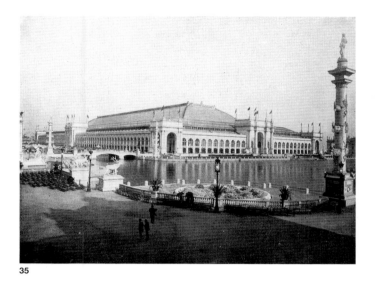

35

36

35 The Manufactures and Liberal Arts Building at the Chicago World's Fair, 1893, designed by George B. Post (1837–1913). This was the largest building of the nineteenth century – it was more than twice the size of the Palais des Machines. Post had been a pupil of Richard M. Hunt, who was the first American graduate of the École des Beaux-Arts. The external architectural treatment is characteristic of the Beaux-Arts in its most banal manifestations.

36 The interior of the Manufactures and Liberal Arts Building at the Chicago World's Fair, 1893: part of the Russian section. Had Dutert not adopted the solution of a double truss at each end of the Palais des Machines, he would have had to resort to a complex corner detail of the kind which can clearly be seen in the photograph.

37 Joining two parts of a truss, the Palais des Machines, Paris Universal Exhibition, 1889. The Fives-Lille Company employed this method of construction, which used pre-assembled components.

21

structure with ogival lattice trusses was J.W. Schwedler's retort shed for the Berliner Imperial-Continental-Gas-Association, which was constructed in 1863. It is plausible to suggest that Dutert also knew of this.[21]

The trusses of the Palais des Machines were to span 110.60 metres – almost precisely a third greater than those of St Pancras. They each incorporated three hinges, which were to compensate for the expansion and contraction of the steel as a result of changes in temperature. These hinges, which were situated at the bases of the trusses and at the meeting point at the apex, were very boldly expressed.

The idea of hinged trusses was not wholly new. In 1858 H.D. Maniton, Chief Engineer of Compagnie du Nord, the railway, used hinged bases for the girders of a 45 metre bridge which crossed the canal at Saint-Denis on the route Paris-Creil. J.W. Schwedler, whose innovative engineering has already been mentioned, designed a three-hinged system for the Unterspree-Brücke, Berlin, of 1864–65.[22]

It is worth pointing out that in 1885–87 G. Herrmann P. Eggert (the architect) and

J.W. Schwedler again (as engineer) used base hinges for the 56 metre span of the train shed of the main station at Frankfurt-am-Main. These base hinges are obfuscated with cast iron ornament of a rather coarse kind, which seems to negate the effect of a considerable weight being transferred to the ground – an effect which Dutert was to fully exploit at the Champ de Mars.

The best account, in English, of the Palais des Machines is to be found in *Engineering*, published on 3 May 1889; it is anonymous. The whole issue of this important weekly journal is devoted to construction at the Paris Universal Exhibition.

Engineering also gives details of other notable metal structures at the exhibition, besides the Palais des Machines. Inevitably, the Eiffel Tower took pride of place. However, the Palais des Arts Libéraux, by Jean-Camille Formigé, was also described in some detail. Like the Palais des Machines, this also had a hinged, or articulated, structure. It is most likely that this feature was introduced by Victor Contamin, Engineer-in-Chief of Metal

Construction who was assisted by Eugène Pierron[23] and Jules-Jean Charton.[24]

Engineering claimed that the Palais des Machines was 'the boldest work in the exhibition, not even excepting the Eiffel Tower … its dimensions exceed anything that has so far been attempted'. Although Dutert was credited solely with the design he was inexplicably described as 'chief engineer'. The Palais des Machines occupied almost the entire width of the Champ de Mars.

Imperial dimensions, were, of course, used in *Engineering*. It covered an area of more than 500,000 square feet; the nave was 363 feet wide and about 1,380 feet long. The side galleries (which I have previously referred to as 'side-chapels') were 57 feet deep. In metric terms, the building covered an area of 48,000 square metres, was 110.6 metres wide, about 421 metres long, and the 'side chapels' were 17.5 metres wide.

But the Palais des Machines was not, in fact, the largest glass-metal building of the nineteenth century. It was to be surpassed in size by the Manufactures and Liberal Arts Building at the Chicago World's Fair of

37

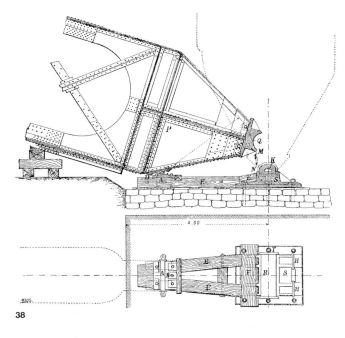

38

1893. This was actually more than twice the size of the Palais des Machines and was 514 metres by 239 metres in plan. The architect was George B. Post, (1837–1913), who had been a pupil of Richard M. Hunt, (1827–95), the first American student of the École des Beaux-Arts. Post's Manufactures and Liberal Arts Building, however, was encased in a plaster architecture of a tame and utterly conventional École des Beaux-Arts kind. It possesses none of the clarity of intention of Dutert's Palais des Machines.

The contract for the construction of the nave of the Palais des Machines was put out to tender on 24 March 1887: the time allowed for construction exceeded that allowed for Paxton's Great Exhibition building by well over a year. The contracts for the side galleries (the 'side chapels') were the subject of four additional contracts which were entered into later. The nave was to be offered to two separate contractors each of whom would be responsible for their own particular half.

The nave was to consist of 19 bays. The bays at each end – the avenue de la Bourdonnais end and the avenue de Suffren end – were to be 24.60 metres, the central bay (which led off to the entrance vestibule) was to be 26.40 metres and the intermediate bays, of which there were eight on either side of the central bay, were to be 21.50 metres. Photographs of the building give an impression of the kind of logical uniformity which was to be associated with Modern Movement structures, but this was not entirely the case, as the foregoing figures indicate.

The end girders, or trusses, were to be double and linked. This made it possible to set back the curtain wall façades at both ends. While the double girders were introduced for obvious structural reasons, recessing the glass façades enabled Dutert to create an impression of a reassuringly solid architectural whole.

The estimated cost of the Palais des Machines was £260,000. A square metre of covered space on the ground thus cost roughly £3.23. In as far as it is possible to 'translate' these figures into current monetary terms (and the exercise is a risky one) these costs appear to have been remarkably reasonable.

As *Engineering* reported: 'After trials made at Chattelerault it was decided to employ steel as the material of the new roof; this is the first time that [this] metal has been used for a work of this kind. The form chosen is that of a surbased ogival [a surbased arch is one of which the rise is less than half the span], the curve being formed of arcs of circles and straight lines … The arch is divided into panels of different sizes. The portion between the two purlins is formed by three small diagonals and two larger ones. This arrangement and division has the advantage of leaving the vertical 10.59 metres apart. Each upright points to the centre of that part of the principal…'.

Engineering records that the contract for the foundations of the Palais des Machines was offered to the public on 20 June 1887 – the total value of this contract according to the estimate was £19,744 with 'caution money' of £800.

While the ground at the Champ de Mars site was generally suitable for a large steel structure, it had been so disturbed by previous exhibition works (the gravel, which had once formed the ancient bed of the Seine, had actually been sold off), some ingenuity was called for in designing the

38 A detail of the base of a truss, the Palais des Machines, 1889. The drawing shows the positioning of a pre-assembled truss on its base hinge by the Fives-Lille Company.
39 The scaffolding system employed by Cail and Company who constructed the half of the Palais des Machines which faced the avenue de Suffren. Drawing after a photograph.

39

40

41

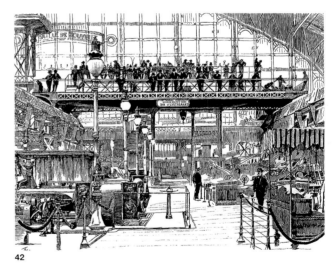

42

40 Building the Palais des Machines, 1889. A sketch of construction workers employed by Cail and Company.

41 The interior, showing the track of one of the *ponts roulants* – this was an electrically powered gantry. The *ponts roulants* were used to put heavy machinery in place during the setting up of the 1889 exhibition; after the exhibition had opened they transported visitors from one end to the other. The section shown in the photograph was devoted to railway equipment.

42 One of the *ponts roulants*, manufactured by Bon and Lustremant for the Paris Universal Exhibition, 1889. Passengers could walk about the 18 metre gantry as if it were the bridge of a ship.

foundations of the giant trusses. Three different types of pier were adopted. Where the alluvial deposits were greater than 3 metres thick the foundation piers consisted of masonry blocks 7 metres long by 3.5 metres wide and 3.65 metres deep; these rested on beds of concrete half-a-metre thick. Of the 40 piers, 25 were of this type. Where the depth of gravel was less, the thickness of the concrete base was increased proportionately. In the cases of those ten piers which had to be constructed on the site of the old gravel pit, piles had to be driven. Remains of foundations from the 1878 exhibition had to be dynamited. Work on the foundations for the Palais des Machines was completed within exactly six months.

Contracts for erecting the nave of the Palais des Machines were awarded to two companies, Fives-Lille, who were responsible for the avenue de la Bourdonnais half; and Cail et Cie., who were commissioned to construct the avenue de Suffren half.

Engineering reported: 'Each of the contractors commenced their work from the centre and advanced towards the gables of the building, but a different method was adopted by each of them … The system followed by the Fives-Lille Company was remarkable for its boldness and simplicity … The plan carried out … was to put together on the ground the ironwork for each girder, in four separate parts and then to raise these into place so that the only riveting up then required was that at the two joints which had to be made … such a system had the advantage of requiring but little scaffolding … all that was employed consisted of a tall central gantry as high as the middle of the roof, and two side platforms. These three gantries were entirely independent of one another, and were mounted on wheels, so that they could be moved forward upon rails … as the work advanced…'.

Considerable ingenuity was shown in the design of the carriages for the scaffolding towers and two sets of wheels were used in order to move the two side carriages laterally. It took two days to move each scaffolding tower to the position of the next truss to be erected. The top and bottom sections of each truss were delivered complete from the Fives-Lille factory while the steel for the intermediate part was delivered unriveted. There were approximately 32,000 rivets in each truss. The first bay was completed in 23 days, the second in 16 days, the third in 12 days and the remainder in ten days each. Fives-Lille employed 250 workers on the project.

Engineering records that 'MM. Cail et Cie. followed an entirely different system … to that followed by the Fives-Lille. It consisted in constructing a narrow scaffolding, the top of which was of the same form as the inner-side of the arch…'.

Riveting was done on the ground and portions of the truss – not exceeding 3 tons in weight – were hauled up into position on the staging places and then riveted to the adjoining pieces. The scaffolding consisted of five towers, each with 12 wheels, which were braced together. This whole construction, with its several working heights, was moved forward from bay to bay. The rails upon which the scaffolding towers ran were portable and had to be re-positioned with meticulous care. Nevertheless, movement from one bay to another was achieved in about an hour and a half, as opposed to the two days of the

43

Fives-Lille system. A daily average of 215 men were employed by Cail et Cie. and the contract was completed within six months.

Both the Fives-Lille and the Cail et Cie. systems had their particular merits and, indeed, were both praised by the Director General of Works, Adolphe Alphand. The 14 per cent saving in manpower by Cail et Cie., over Fives-Lille, did not pass unnoticed by contemporaries. But it was the semi-prefabricated method of Fives-Lille which accords more with our own approach to construction.

The Entrance to the Palais des Machines

The main entrance to the Palais des Machines was from the Palais des Sections Industrielles – with Bouvard's gaudy dome marking the entrance. But, nevertheless, the Palais des Machines was dignified with its own monumental entry – albeit one which existed mainly as an interior. It was described as the Grand Vestibule. It was a domed structure and was designed by Dutert himself. The 25.7 metre diameter dome was supported on four large wrought iron stanchions which were 22 metres in height. In plan the Grand Vestibule

measured 30 metres by 36.8 metres.

The ceiling of the dome of the Grand Vestibule was glazed. It was divided into 16 large segments filled with coloured leaded glass. At night these were back-lit by powerful electric lamps. The idea was almost certainly without precedent. Could it, perhaps, have been the inspiration for Bruno Taut's famous Glashaus at the Deutsche Werkbund Exhibition at Cologne in 1914?

The Grand Vestibule was highly decorated – 'florid' thought *Engineering*. So too, was the Palais des Machines itself. It is the presence of this decoration, I suspect, which, in the past, led to a degree of confusion concerning who was the actual designer of the building.

Contamin, the engineer, could all too easily be hailed as the previously unsung hero of the occasion. Conversely, Dutert, the architect, could be demonized as the desperate purveyor of Beaux-Arts decorative nostrums – irrelevant antefixes[25] on the gables and meaningless plaster ornament, wherever it could be applied: all this on a building dedicated to the machine. The defamatory view is, of

course, no longer acceptable. (Post-modernism, if it has taught us little about the real function of ornament, has at least rendered us more susceptible to its blandishments.) And like that of another champion of both advanced structural technology and traditional architectural culture – Otto Wagner – Dutert's reputation stands as high as it has ever done.

Dutert, in his design of the Palais des Machines, was able to synthesize a number of traditions. These traditions have already been touched upon. But, in assessing the significance of Dutert's achievement, it is necessary to refer to them again.

Firstly, there was the École des Beaux-Arts tradition, of which Dutert was among the most accomplished of exponents. This tradition was simultaneously historicist and forward-looking. In terms of approved models, the Classical was invariably preferred above all others. But Beaux-Arts Classicism involved what may be described as the creative restoration of antiquity.[26] Polychromatic restoration – based upon the belief that Greek architecture had been brilliantly coloured – formed an important part of the Beaux-Arts approach to

43 The entrance to the Palais des Machines at the avenue de la Bourdonnais end. An allegorical sculpture made of plaster representing Electricity. The sculptor was Louis Ernest-Barries.

44 A large automatic lathe by Greenwood and Batley Ltd, Leeds, displayed in the British section of the Palais des Machines. Machinery such as this had considerable potential in the armaments industry.

45 The Palais des Machines entrance from the avenue de la Bourdonnais. The colouring of the steel work was described as *"d'un ton légèrement rosé"* – a yellow shade lightly tinged with pink. (It contrased with the typical blue-grey of contemporary iron structures in France.) The stained glass window incorporated the coats of arms of Marseille, Lyon, Lille, Bordeaux, Washington, London, St Petersburg, Vienna, Peking, Tokyo, Rio de Janeiro... The arched and polychromatic entrance in Louis Sullivan's Transportation Building, Chicago World's Fair, 1893, may owe a little to the Palais des Machines.

44

46

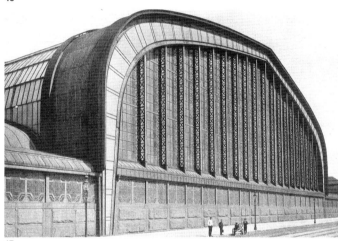

47

Classicism.[27] Dutert certainly applied polychromatic principles to the colouring of both the interior and exterior of the Palais des Machines.

Beaux-Arts Classicism, while it could be stultifying, could on many occasions give rise to, in the hands of those who were not intimidated by antiquity, an architecture which was appropriate to a society in which industrial growth was accelerating almost exponentially. One thinks particularly of the architecture of Labrouste (and his pupil Louis-Ernest Lheureux), Garnier and Dutert.

Secondly, there was the tradition (if tradition it can be called) of Viollet-le-Duc's modernized Gothic. This appealed to France, in something of the same way that Pugin's Gothic had done to Britain. Gothic could be presented as being 'Northern', that is, having its origins in Northern Europe. This thought of a specifically Northern architecture satisfied not only those for whom national sentiments were important, but also those who wished to defer to science. There was a kind of Darwinian inevitability in Gothic. The Gothicizing elements in Dutert's Palais des Machines were there for all to see – and not only Huysmans noticed them. But they were so well digested that historians have only recently actually begun to pay attention to them.

Thirdly, there was the newly important matter of technology as a significant architectural determinant. Technology was advancing at near breakneck pace when Dutert designed the Palais des Machines. It was to be expected that he would be influenced by this process. Soon the paradigm would shift from steam to electricity.

Some of the train-shed precursors of the Palais des Machines have been referred to, the most important of which was St Pancras Station by Barlow and Ordish of 1868. There was also the gigantic Firth of Forth Bridge (by John Fowler, Benjamin Baker and William Arrol). The Forth Bridge was begun five years before the Palais des Machines and, like it, was also completed in 1889. Its heroic scale must surely have inspired Dutert, and those associated with him, to do for architecture what had been done for civil engineering.

The Palais des Machines was quite definitely a work of architecture – unlike the

48

49 The demolition of the Palais des Machines, 1909.
50 The demolition, 1909. The form of the 'side chapels' can be seen clearly. The famous ferris wheel is in the background.
51 The demolition of the Palace of Fine Arts, 1909.

27

49

50

51

Crystal Palace, which was to be elevated to the status of architecture only retrospectively. In consequence, the Palais des Machines passed into the collective unconsciousness of a generation of turn-of-the-century architects. One can see its ogival roof form, for example, in Joseph Maria Olbrich's little temporary wooden pavilion for the fine arts at the Darmstadt Exhibition of 1901. Olbrich used a similar ogival roof form again for his projected sign for the train shed of the main station at Basel of 1903.[28]

The main station for Hamburg designed by Reinhardt and Süssenguth, which was illustrated in the *Werkbund Jahrbuch* for 1914, with its braced curtain wall and its ogee-shaped trusses, is even closer to the Palais des Machines. A reasonable case could be made that the model factory by Walter Gropius at the Werkbund Exhibition at Cologne in 1914 also bears a passing resemblance to the Palais des Machines. In the era before the First World War, Dutert's building was a legend and it had left traces in architectural memories. Peter Behrens's Turbine Hall of 1910, built for

AEG, in Berlin, with its curtain walls and its hinged trusses, may also be cited.

The Palais des Machines was the product of an architectural culture of great refinement and sophistication. This culture was mediated by the École des Beaux-Arts. Dutert perfectly understood its rules and how these might be adapted to modern circumstances.

Dutert was able to respond to the challenge of his turbulent and optimistic era. The Palais des Machines, with its many historical references, is evidence that intelligent and judicious historicism may have an entirely benign influence upon architecture.

The polarities of industrialization – which promised dangers as well as benefits – were nowhere more apparent than in the Paris of 1889. This is the particular cultural context of the Palais des Machines. It is, in consequence, far more than a mere example of an important historical building-type. It is representative of a pivotal moment in the collective history of the modern world. This can be said of very few buildings, indeed, perhaps, no other.

52 A detail of the base of one of the trusses of Formigé's Palais des Arts Libéraux, Paris Universal Exhibition, 1889. It would seem likely that Victor Contamin was responsible for this detail, which was more or less replicated in the Palais des Machines.

53 A photograph of the interior of the Palais des Machines taken in 1889 before the installation of the exhibits. The central space was 110 metres by 420 metres; the subsidiary structures or 'side chapels' were 17.5 metres deep.

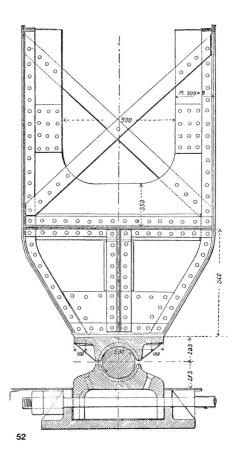

52

53

54

30

54 The interior of the Palais des Machines looking towards the staircase to the upper gallery on the side facing the avenue de la Motte Piquet and the École Militaire. The arms of Rouen, Nantes, Paris, Toulouse and St Etienne can be seen above the stained glass window with the signs of the Zodiac. Decorations such as these prompted certain Modernist historians to relegate Dutert to an 'associated architect'.

55 The avenue de la Bourdonnais façade. Dutert's original intention had been to have three large chimneys at each corner but the advances in technology made it possible for the exhibits to be powered electrically at generating stations situated inconspicuously in the exhibition.

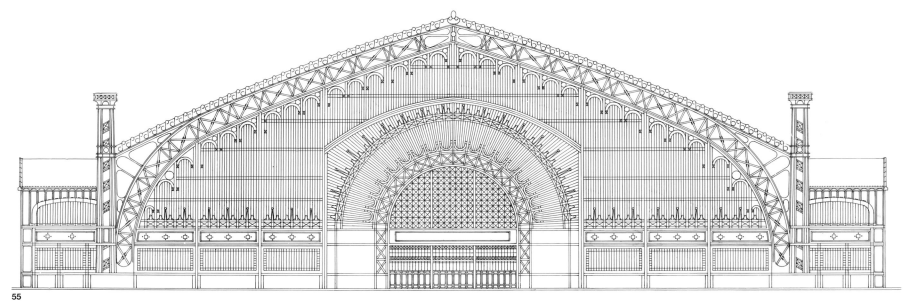

55

0   15m
0   40ft

56 A bronze fountain by
Frédéric-Auguste Bartholdi,
in the Grand Vestibule, 1889.

31

32 **57** Ferdinand Dutert, section
through the Grand Vestibule –
the entrance from the exhibition
itself to the Palais des Machines,
1889.
58 Ferdinand Dutert, plan, seen
from below, of the cupola of the
Grand Vestibule, of the Palais
des Machines, 1889.

57

34

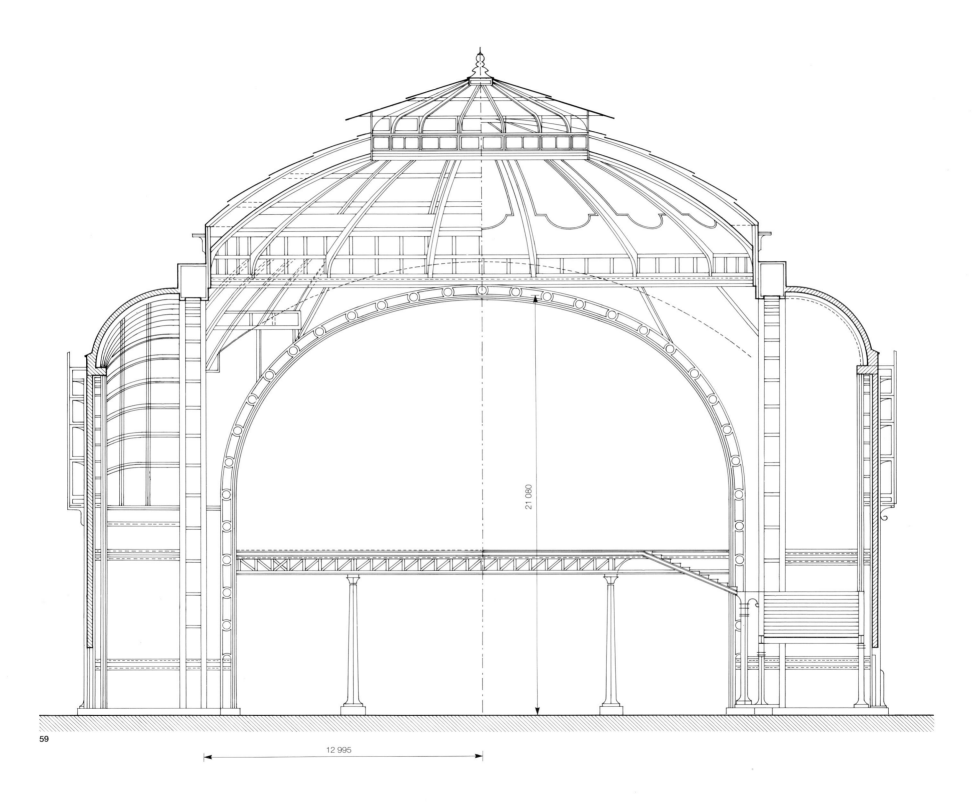

59

0   3m

0   10ft

60 An elevation showing details of the three forms of the sub-sidiary structures ('side chapels'), 1889. The tower on the right (at the avenue de Suf-fren end) is less tall than those on the avenue de la Bourdonnais end. Originally three tall chim-neys were to have been built at each corner.

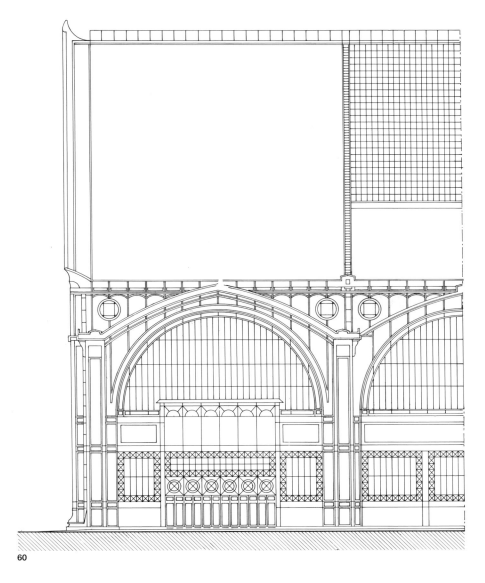

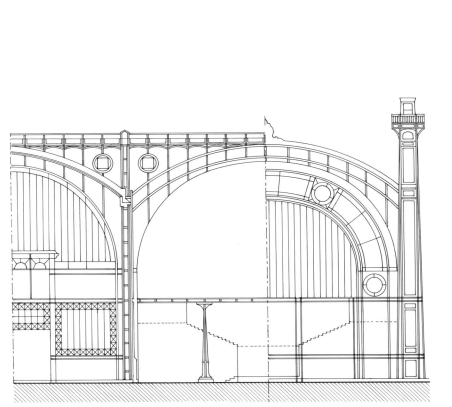

60

0 ⊢———⊣ 5m
0 ⊢————————⊣ 15ft

61

62

61 Ferdinand Dutert, perspective showing the cupola of the Grand Vestibule with the 'Galerie de 30 mètres' in the background. This gallery led directly to Bouvard's Dôme Central, the focal point of the 1889 exhibition.

62 Wrought iron details for the main staircase of Dutert's for the Palais des Machines, 1889. Dutert was very accomplished in the design of decorative details.

38

63 An interior view of the Palais des Machines showing the British Section.

64 An interior view, looking towards the avenue de Suffren end. The tracks of the two *ponts roulants* can be seen clearly. Below these ran the rotative shafts which drove the machines with canvas belts.

65 An interior view, looking towards the avenue de Suffren end, showing the Swiss section in the foreground.

66 The Swiss section, 1889.

63

64

65

66

67

68

67 The interior of the Palais des Machines, looking towards the avenue de la Bourdonnais. The deck of one of the *ponts roulants* can clearly be seen on the right.

68 The stained-glass curtain wall can be seen at the avenue de Suffren end. The tower was used for viewing the machinery in operation.

40

69 A view of the first floor gallery. The stencilled decoration of the ceilings of the 'side chapels' is comparatively simple. The more ceremonial parts of the building had elaborate gilded and painted plaster.

70 A view of the American section on the first floor.

71 The first floor gallery.

72 A detail of the hinged base of one of the trusses, published in *Engineering*, 3 May 1889.

73 A view towards the avenue de Suffren end. Photographs such as this prompted historians like Pevsner and Hitchcock to interpret the building in terms of the Modern Movement.

69

70

71

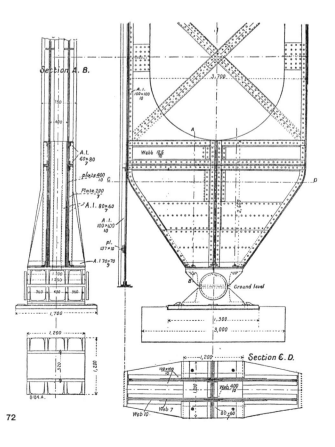

72

42 **74** The method of supporting pre-assembled trusses with timber balks during the construction of the Palais des Machines, 1889, as used by the Fives-Lille Company.
75 The method of erecting the trusses of the Palais des Machines as used by the Fives-Lille Company.
76 A proposed method of erecting complete trusses. This method was not employed as the weights were too great.
77 The scaffolding system employed by Cail and Company. This method, which suited the technology of the era, was probably the most effective.

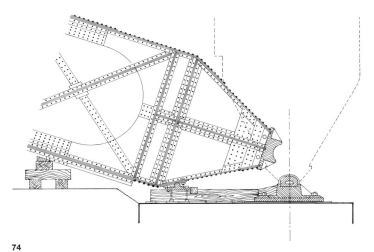

74

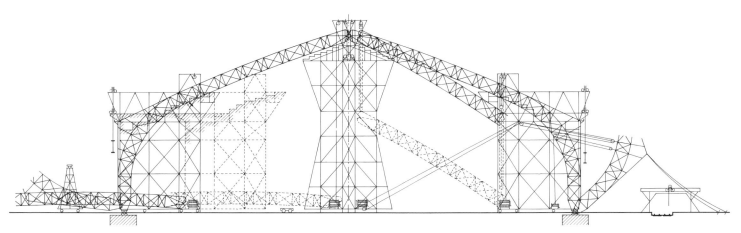

75

76

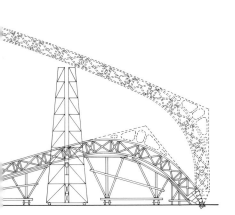

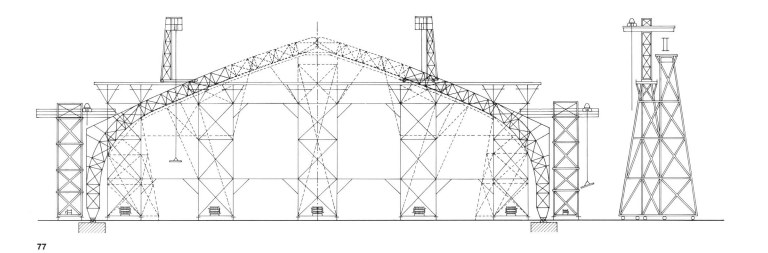

78, 79 Chromolithographic
illustrations of coloured plaster
decorations on the ceiling of the
Palais des Machines, 1889.
From the monograph by
Adolphe Alphand, Director of
Works at the Paris Universal
Exhibition.

LOIRET

ORLEANS

LILLE

80 The display by the Marinoni printing company in the Palais des Machines, 1889. Marinoni were the printers of the illustrated journal *Le Figaro*. The machines were fully functioning and their operatives can be seen in attendance. Above the platform Marinoni display the embarkation for one of the *ponts roulants*. Its track can also be seen.

81 The working lighthouse in the centre of the Palais des Machines, 1889.

82 A display of portable steam engines.

83 The Gallery of Machines, foreign section, at the Universal Exhibition, Paris 1900. During the 1900 exhibition Dutert's Palais des Machines was used for the display of food products.

80

81

82

83

48   **84** Ferdinand Dutert, Design for decorations for the Palais des Machines. Ink with sepia wash. The transformation of mechanical elements into classicizing ornament should be noted in some of these designs.

84

Plan
The Grand Vestibule, the main entry to the Palais des Machines, can be seen at the bottom. The avenue de la Bourdonnais entrance is to the left; the avenue de Suffren is to the right. Above are the avenue de la Motte Piquet and the École Militaire.

Drawings

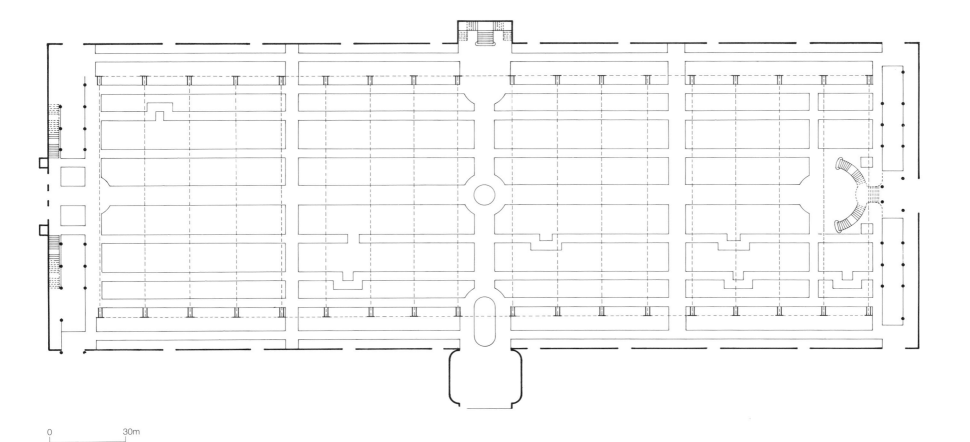

0   30m

0   100ft

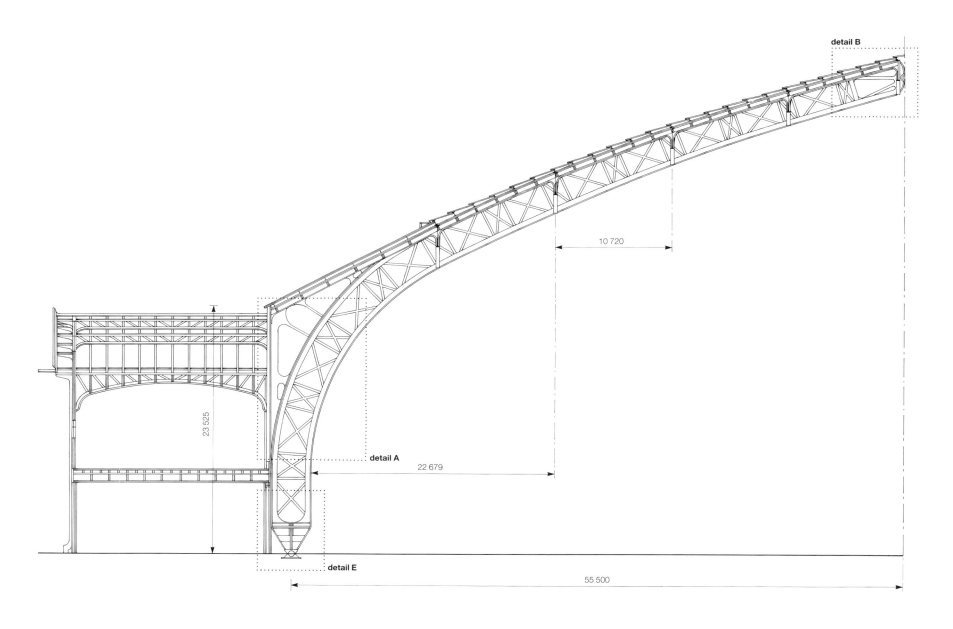

50 **Cross section**
The main trusses span a total of
111 metres (360 feet).

detail B

10 720

23 525

detail A
22 679

detail E

55 500

0   10m

0   30ft

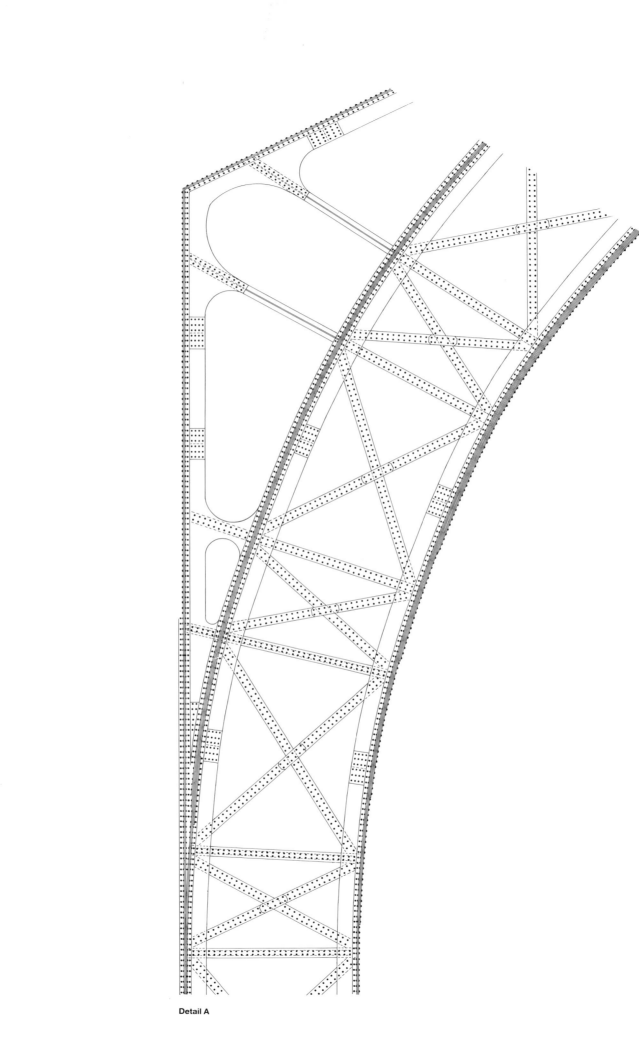

Truss detail
The trusses and subsidiary
structural elements are of
riveted steel.

Detail A

0   2m

0   5ft

Truss head detail

Pin joints are located at the
base and apex of each pair of
trusses to allow for differential
movement.

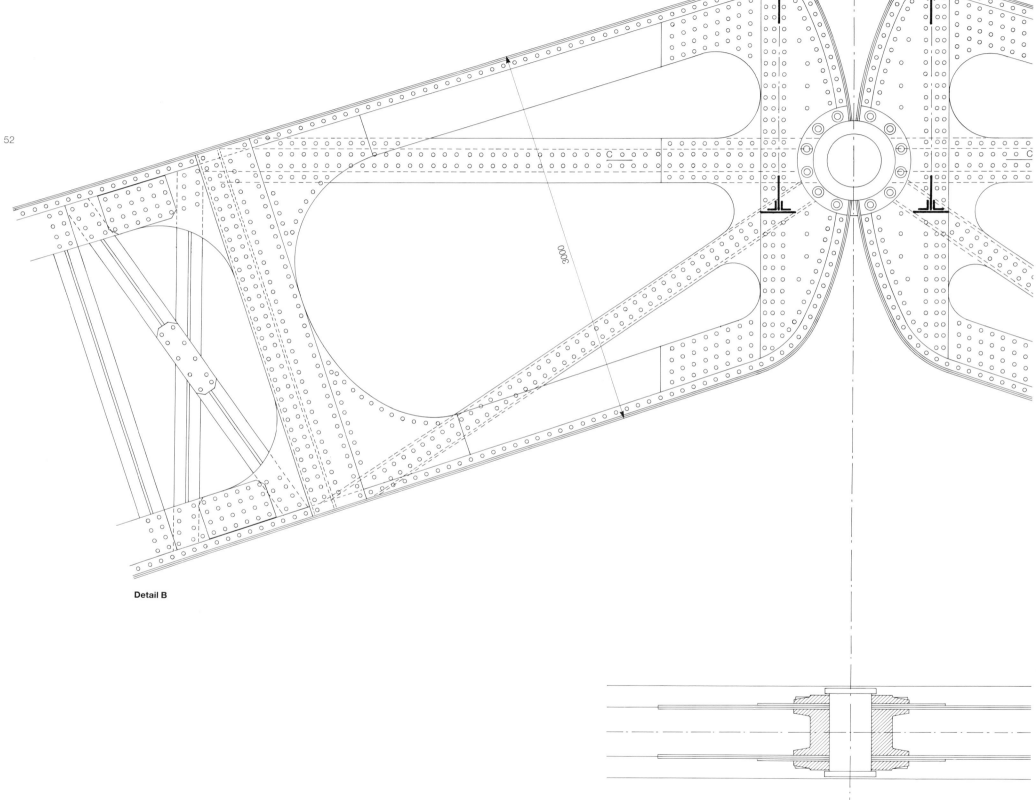

3000

Detail B

Section CC

0   500mm

0   18in

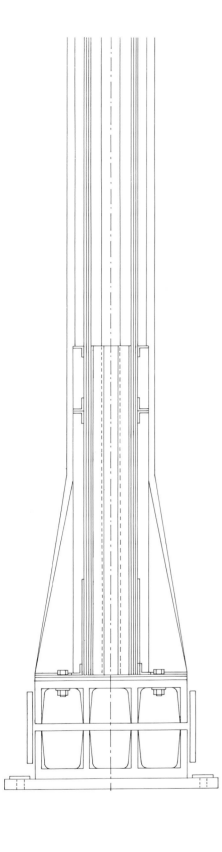

Section DD

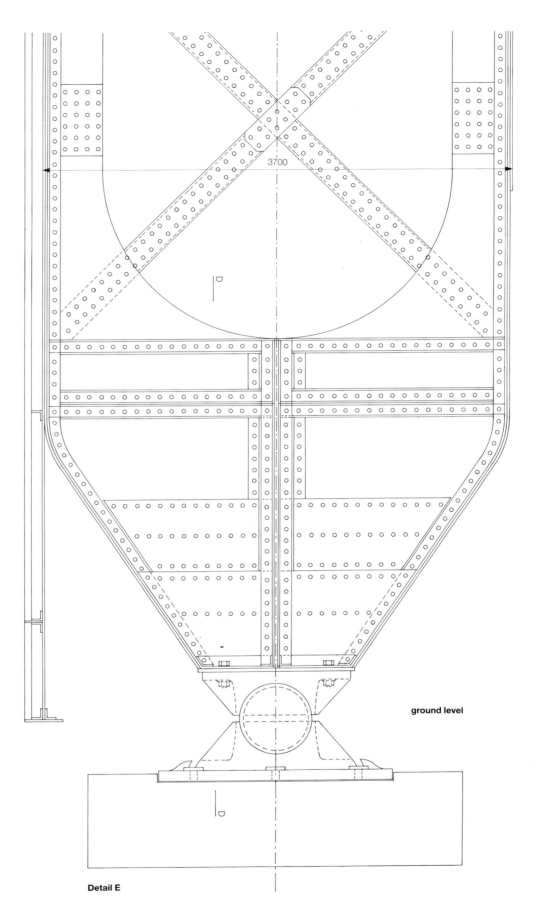

3700

Truss base detail

In certain early illustrations Dutert appears to have treated the bases of the trusses in a more conventionally 'architectural' manner.

ground level

Detail E

54 **Elevation**
Details of the three forms of
the subsidiary structures ('side
chapels'). Left, a typical bay,
centre, the central bay, right,
the end bay – with additional
bracing.

0   5m

0   15ft

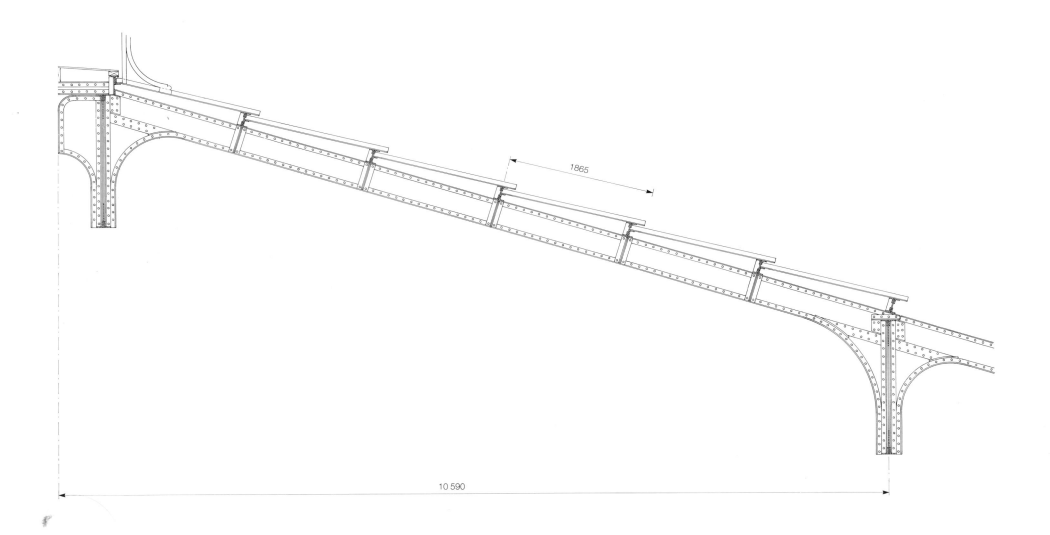

1865

10 590

0   1m

0   3ft

A Structural Appraisal

Angus Low, MA CEng MICE

The structure of the Palais des Machines proclaims the confidence of its age. Dutert and Contamin would have been aware that its span exceeded that of any previous building by 52 per cent. This was a leap which far exceeded the shuffling steps of an evolutionary process and it is an indication of their confidence in their own understanding of structural theory. Looking back with the benefit of a further hundred years of developments in both theory and practice, the overwhelming impression is that their confidence was justified. They produced a well conceived and elegant design.

The main element of the design is the trussed arch which, with some variations, was repeated 20 times, dividing the 421m length of the building into 19 structural bays. It was the 111m span of this arch which was the principal technical achievement. This span was made possible by the use of steel, a new material at that time, which was gradually replacing wrought iron. The specification for the steel used matches in yield strength, breaking strength and ductility one of the grades in the latest European standards for steel. The

material was good but the production process limited the thickness of the plate. The thickest elements were of 10mm plate but many were only 7mm thick. Where the forces were large, up to six plates were bound together with rivets. An advantage of the thin plates is that the steps in the section thicknesses would have been barely perceptible.

From the geometry of the arch, a number of the intentions of the designers can be inferred. The Gothic form of the arch truss results in a pitched roof which would help to shed snow. A three-pinned articulation of the arch is achieved with cylindrical pin bearings at the crown and at the two arch springings which produce the maximum visual impact by being exactly at floor level. This articulation would have been introduced to channel the resultant thrust within the arch along a predetermined trajectory, shown as a double line in figure 1, and hence would have released any restraint forces due to temperature expansion and contraction.

Away from the crown the pitch steepens gradually as the roof line describes a gentle curve. This curve follows the general trend

of the force trajectory and so reduces the forces in the truss members. The diagonal members within the truss form a distinctive pattern of alternating major and minor bays with the size of the minor bays gradually increasing. The purpose of this is to provide true verticals within the truss at regular centres across the roof to which the longitudinal trusses of the roof can be fixed.

The arch form deviates furthest from the force trajectory where it curves past the eaves and so this is where the forces on the truss are greatest. To resist these forces the strength of the members is increased with multiple plate thicknesses and the depth of the truss is increased. The increase is introduced gradually all the way from the crown. The curve of the truss continues until its axis is vertical just above the springing. The force trajectory never becomes steeper than about 30 degrees to the vertical. The verticality is imposed on the arches to allow unobstructed use of the floorspace around their springings and to enhance the visual lightness of the structure.

The designers would have known how to calculate the forces in a triangulated truss.

They would probably have used a graphical construction drawn out on paper. They would have realized that the crossed diagonals introduced some redundancy into the system which would invalidate their method but they would have had some conventional procedures to follow to circumvent this problem. For the pattern of forces calculated, they would have selected an arrangement of cover plates which would give each member a sufficient cross-sectional area to keep the stresses within the required limits. From the data available today a computer analysis has been used to recreate these calculations. Figure 1 shows the line diagram of the computer model together with the calculated force trajectory. For the eaves region Figure 2 shows the magnitude of the axial forces plotted along each member under the building's own weight together with the design snow load. Figure 3 shows the area of cross-sections of the steel members, including their cover-plates, deduced from the drawings. Figure 4 shows the distribution of the resulting stress, the force per unit area. The point to note is that despite a marked variation in the forces in

1 Half an arch with the calculated thrust line for maximum vertical load.
2 The eaves region showing axial forces plotted along each member.
3 The areas of the cross-sections of the steel members plotted along each member.
4 The axial stress in the steel plotted along each member.

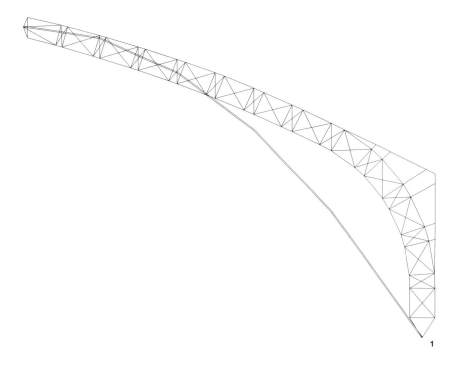

1

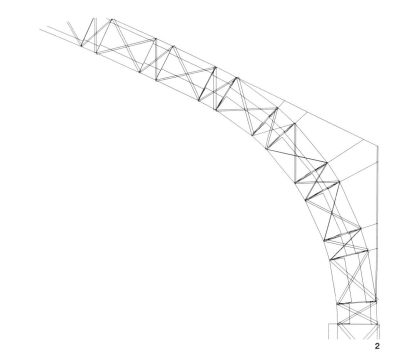

2

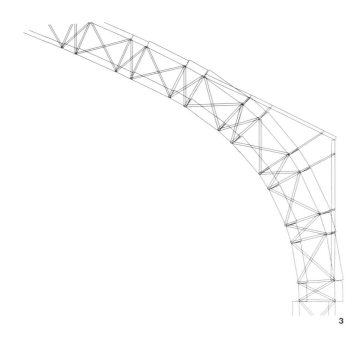

3

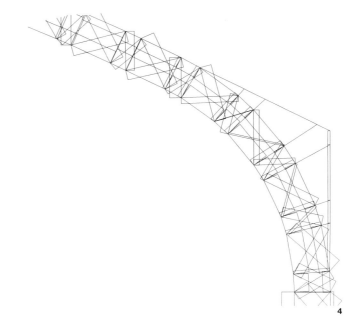

4

members the pattern of cover plates results in a fairly uniform stress of just less than 100 megapascals (1020 kg/cm² or 6.47 tons per square inch) in all the plated members. The conclusion from this exercise is that the designer's calculations gave a similar distribution of forces to those found with a modern computer analysis. Modern structural codes would allow this steel to be worked at a stress of about 155 megapascals but the calculation has not allowed for deductions for rivet holes, so the difference is smaller.

The discussion above considers the safety of the structure against the yielding of the elements. It concerns the strength of the steel. Contamin and Dutert would probably have felt less confident when considering the possibility of a buckling failure in one of the trusses. This concerns the flexibility of steel elements in compression. The flexibility of the steel material would have been well known but they would not have been able to quantify the consequences of this flexibility when introduced into different configurations of trusses. They would have known that the problems would be disproportionately

greater for a larger structure and they would have been very conscious of the magnitude of the step they were proposing. Buckling is avoided by restraining a truss at close enough centres. The trusses of the main arches are restrained at 10.7m centres by the longitudinal trusses. The report of the design published in *Engineering* in May 1889 says that the decision to use steel was made after trials at Chattelerault. It is likely that these trials consisted of load tests on full-sized sections of the arch to assess its buckling resistance. Without knowing more details of the form of the connections it is not possible to assess the design in accordance with current practice but nineteeth-century engineers were generally less cautious in their treatment of buckling than we are today.

To this day steel erectors discuss the pros and cons of building 'piece large' or 'piece small'. The former means that large pieces of structure are assembled at ground level and then a large capacity crane is used to lift them into their required position. In contrast, the latter only needs a small crane but the assembly operations must be simple enough to be carried out

safely in difficult conditions at a height. Clearly this debate has lasted for over a century because the construction of the steelwork for the Palais des Machines was let in two contracts and one contractor opted to build 'piece large' and the other chose 'piece small'. No cranes were used. Pieces were lifted by means of a pulley system suspended from timber towers and operated through winches which required up to 12 men to work them. For the 'piece large' construction quarter sections of the whole arch, each weighing up to 48 tonnes, were lifted onto timber towers. For the 'piece small' operation a timber scaffold was built under the full extent of one arch and the largest lift was only 3 tonnes. Both contractors built their scaffolds on wheels so they could be rolled forward to the next arch.

In visualizing the alternative erection methods, it is important to remember that the dominant activity would have been rivetting. To modern eyes this would have been terrifying but to those recording the proceedings it was so normal that they did not mention it. The rivets were heated in a furnace until the steel was red hot and quite

soft. The furnace would be big and heavy and would probably be situated at ground level. Without having time to cool the rivets were thrown to the team on the scaffold consisting of a catcher, a placer and two hammer men who would strike the two ends simultaneously. The resulting connections were strong because the rivets contracted on cooling and provided a very firm clamping force. Today such practices are prohibited by safety legislation.

Looking back across a hundred years the concept of the design and the understanding of the forces involved look fairly familiar. It is the construction methods that belong to a different age.

58

Acknowledgements & Sources

The author would like to thank Alan Kent, Librarian, Faculty of Design, Kingston University, for allowing the use of material in the University's Special Collection, and Elizabeth Darling, Kingston University.

1, 4, 32, 33, 34, 41, 49, 50, 51, 54, 63–66, 81–83: Roger-Viollet, Paris

2, 3, 9, 39, 40, 42, 80: reproduced from F.G.Dumas and L.De Fourcaud, *Revue de l'Exposition* (Paris, 1889)

5: reproduced from E.E.Viollet-le-Duc, *Entretiens sur l'Architecture* (Paris, 1863)

6: reproduced from *Les Grands Prix de Rome d'Architecture de 1850 à 1900. École Nationale des Beaux-Arts Cinquantaire* (Paris, n.d.)

7: Musée d'Orsay, Paris/photo R.M.N., Paris

8: Musée d'Orsay, Paris (Fonds Eiffel)/photos R.M.N., Paris

10, 11, 27: The Victoria & Albert Museum, London

12, 14, 21, 23, 24, 37: reproduced from *L'Exposition de Paris* (Paris, 1888–90), Kingston University Special Collection

13: reproduced from *Le Monde Illustré* (June 16, 1888), Bibliothèque Nationale, Paris

15, 17, 18, 20, 22, 25, 26, 30, 31, 38, 52, 55, 59, 60, 72, 74–77: *Engineering* (May 3, 1889)

16, 48, 68: reproduced from *Figaro Exposition* (Paris & London, 1889)

19, 53, front cover: Studio Chevojon, Paris

28: Central Photographic Unit, British Railways Board

29: reproduced from E.E.Viollet-le-Duc, *Encyclopédie d'Architecture Revue Mensuelle* (Paris, 1872–77)

35, 36: reproduced from *The Columbian Gallery. A Portfolio of Photographs from The World's Fair* (Chicago, 1894)

43, 67, 70, 71: Bibliothèque Historique de la Ville de Paris/photo G.Leyris

44: reproduced from Glucq, *L'Album de l'Exposition* (Paris, 1889)

45, 62, 78, 79: reproduced from A. Alphand, *Exposition Universelle Internationale de 1889, monographie* (Paris, 1892)

46, 47: reproduced from *Jahrbuch des Deutschen Werkbundes* (Jena, 1914)

56: École Nationale Supérieure des Beaux-Arts, Paris

57, 58, 61, 84: Musée de la Chartreuse, Douai

69, 73: Bibliothèque des Arts Décoratifs, Paris/photo Jean-Loup Charmet

Structural Appraisal 1, 2, 3, 4: produced by the computing facilities of the Ove Arup Partnership

Palais des Machines: dimensions

Span, principal trusses: 110.60m
Height: 43.50m
Length: 420.00m
Width of side galleries: 17.50m
Height of side galleries: 22.5m
Height of first floor in side galleries: 8.00m
Total floor area: 80.400 sq.m
According to Tancrède Martel (see Bibliography) the Palais des Machines could accommodate an army corps of 30,000 men, or 12,000 cavalrymen and their horses, with the cavalrymen sleeping on the first floor.

Notes

1 See Louis Rousselet, *L'Exposition universelle de 1889*, Paris, 1895.
2 See Roland Barthes, 'The Eiffel Tower', in *The Eiffel Tower and other Mythologies* (trans. Richard Howell), New York, 1979.
3 See Tancrède Martel, 'Le Palais des Machines', in *Revue de l'Exposition Universelle de 1889* (eds F.G. Dumas and L. De Fourcaud), Paris, 1889.
4 Quoted also by Marie-Laure Crosnier Leconte in 'La Galerie des Machines', in *1889. La Tour Eiffel et l'Exposition Universelle*, Paris, 1989 (catalogue of the centenary exhibition at the Musée d'Orsay). The passage is reproduced more or less in its entirety below. It is taken from J.K. Huysmans, *Certains*, Paris, 1889.
'The interior of this palace is truly splendid … a colossal hall … taller than the highest of cathedral naves. It rises up on delicate vaults … giant ogees, which resolve the vertiginous downward thrusts – all under an endless sea of glass. And in this immense, apparently half empty, space are the machines – dwarfed and now become all too mundane, despite the lewd gestures they make when they are in motion.
'The form of this chamber is inspired by Gothic constructional virtuosity, but here it is surpassed … it could never be constructed in stone … its supports are great communion-chalice shaped arches.
'At night, when the Edison lamps are lit, the hall appears to expand and become infinite … this palace then becomes magical … from the point of view of art, this hall constitutes the most impressive achievement which the metal industry has yet accomplished.
'Only, as with the Hippodrome and the Bibliothèque Nationale … all the effect is entirely internal … it is ineffective if judged by its exterior… Architecture. therefore, has not actually taken such a new step: lacking a man of genius, iron is still as yet incapable of nurturing an entirely personal production of a single mind, an authentic masterpiece.'
See also J.K. Huysman's 'Promenades à l'Exposition', in *Revue de l'Exposition Universelle de 1889* (eds F.G. Dumas and L. De Fourcaud), Paris, 1889, which contains a shorter version of this passage.
5 Victor Contamin was born in Paris in 1840 and educated at the École Centrale from which he graduated in 1860. He began his career in Barcelona as director of a gas manufacturing plant. After returning to Paris he became a draughtsman in the office of the permanent-way department of the Compagnie des Chemins de Fer du Nord. His work on hoists and bridges was greatly admired and his progress was rapid. He ended his career as Chief Engineer of the company in 1890. Contamin was a distinguished teacher and taught at the École Centrale, where he was Lecturer in Mechanics from 1864 to 1872; he held the Chair of Applied Resistance from 1873 to 1891. In 1878 his lectures were published as *Cours de Resistance Appliquée*. The greatest achievement of his career was to be his nomination as Engineer in Chief of Metal Constructions (Ingenieur en Chef des Constructions Métalliques) for the Exposition Universelle of 1889, by Edouard Lockroy, the Minister of Commerce and Industry. He was assisted by Jules-Jean Charton (d.1921) and Eugène Pierron (1848–98), also graduates of the École Centrale, in the calculations of the stresses of all the metal structures in the Exposition Universelle. Contamin died at Le Vésinet at the age of 53.
See *1889. La Tour Eiffel et l'Exposition Universelle*, Paris, 1989 (catalogue of the centenary exhibition at the Musée d'Orsay).
6 This is quoted by Raymond McGrath and A.C. Frost in *Glass in Architecture and Decoration*, London, 1937.
7 The relevant passage is quoted here in full: 'Over-impressed, perhaps, by the more functional engineering feat of construction at the 1889 Exhibition provided by the wide-spanned metal-and-glass Palais des Machines of the engineers Contamin (1840–93), Pierron and Charton – in which the contribution of the associated architect C.L.F. Dutert (1845–1906) was relatively unimportant – certain later critics have preferred that structure to the Eiffel Tower.' Henry-Russel Hitchcock, *Architecture: Nineteenth and Twentieth Centuries*, Harmondsworth, 1958, p.283.
8 Victor Blavette became a student of the École des Beaux-Arts in 1869, at the age of 19. He joined the atelier of Constant-Dufeux and later that of Ginain. He was winner of the École's Second Grand Prix in 1878 with a design for a cathedral. In the following year he won the Premier Grand Prix with a design for a music conservatoire. During his time in Italy he made measured drawings of the Doge's Palace in Venice. In 1884, he produced a set of fine polychromatic restoration drawings of the Doric Sanctuary at Eleusis which were much admired and he was awarded a Première Medaille at the Salon of 1885.
Blavette's talents were widely recognized and it is not surprising that Dutert chose him as Inspector for the Palais des Machines. Later, as Architect in Chief of Bâtiments Civils et Palais Nationaux, Blavette was responsible for major monuments like the extensions to the Musée d'Histoire Naturelle (by Dutert) the Louvre and the Tuileries. He succeeded Julien Guadet as Professor of Architectural Theory at the École des Beaux-Arts – a post which he held until the age of 78. He died at the age of 83.
See *Paris – Rome – Athènes. Le Voyage en Grèce des Architectes Français aux XIXe et XXe Siècles*, Paris, 1982.
9 *Entretiens sur l'Architecture* was published between 1863 and 1872. However, it is the accompanying *Atlas* (dated 1864 on the title page) which contains the superbly drawn plates of modernized Gothic, which were to be so influential. These are pl.xix – stone and brick vaulting supported by intermediary cast-iron columns; pl.xxi – a market hall supported on angled cast-iron columns (which was the inspiration for Hector Guimard's École du Sacré Coeur of 1895); pl.xxii – a complex hemispherical and square vaulted roofing system supported on angled cast-iron columns, the bases of which are linked by numerous wrought-iron ties; pls xxiii and xxiv – hôtels de ville, with many cast and wrought iron decorative and structural external details; pls xxv and xxvi – large scale vaulting in iron; pl. xxxv – the rear elevation of a town house which has a small brick bay (restrained by angle-irons) to accommodate a staircase, supported on a cast-iron column; pl.xxxvi – an emporium with a glazed tile façade and exposed iron structural ties (the inspiration for Jules Saulnier's Chocolat Menier factory, Noisel sur Marne, 1871–72).

Robin Middleton and David Watkin cite the Bibliothèque de l'École de Droit, Paris, 1876–78, by Louis-Ernest Lheureux (1827–98), a pupil of Henri Labrouste, as betraying the influence of Viollet-le-Duc. See Robin Middleton and David Watkin, *Neoclassical and Nineteenth Century Architecture /2*, London, 1987.

10 See Neil Levine, 'The book and the building: Hugo's theory of architecture and Labrouste's Bibliothèque Ste-Geneviève' in *The École des Beaux-Arts and nineteenth-century French architecture* (ed. Robin Middleton), London, 1984, pp.139–73.

Levine's conclusion, although perhaps tendentious, captures the intellectual zeitgeist: 'By 1830 no other machine could have been said to have affected communication so profoundly as the printing-press and thus to have explained the ever-decreasing sphere of architecture's influence. The analogy of the printed book allowed architecture to break out of the confines of classicism and develop a functional form of expression, and thus ever since Hugo declared the death of architecture as society's principal means of expression, the issue has been to make architecture out of building'.

11 Details of the Universal Exhibition of 1889 are taken from a variety of contemporary sources, which are listed in the bibliography. An additional and obviously invaluable source has been the catalogue of the exhibition celebrating the 1889 Centenary Exhibition at the Musée d'Orsay: *1889. La Tour Eiffel et l'Exposition Universelle*, Paris, 1989.

12 Charles Garnier (1825–98) became an Elève of the École des Beaux-Arts in the atelier of Lebas, which was also to be Dutert's atelier. He was, like Dutert, a Prix de Rome winner – with a design, of 1848, for a Conservatoire des Arts et Métiers. He is best known for his design of the Paris Opéra (1862–75) – the ideal exemplar of the style of the Second Empire. Garnier played an important role in the organization of the Universal Exhibition of 1889 as architectural adviser (architecte conseil de l'Exposition). He was responsible for the historical section which told the story of the evolution of human dwellings with elaborate and frequently fanciful reconstructions of primitive and ancient houses – an idea which had been suggested by Viollet-le-Duc's *Histoire de l'Habitation Humaine depuis les Temps Préhistoriques jusqu'à Nos Jours*, Paris, 1875.

13 Jean-Camille Formigé (1845–1926) intended initially to become a painter. However, he joined the Beaux-Arts atelier of C. Laisne in 1865. He was responsible for some of the most important buildings of the Universal Exhibition of 1889. These were the Palais des Beaux-Arts and the Palais des Arts Libéraux as well as the smaller Galerie Desaix and the Galerie Rapp. Formigé spoke the same stylistic language as Dutert, although with less moderation.

14 See *Exposition Publique des Produits de l'Industrie Française. Catalogue des Produits Industriels*, Paris, an VII (1798). Clockmakers, manufacturers of porcelain, chemical products, manufacturers of artists' materials (including Conté, the crayon manufacturer), wallpaper manufacturers etc. exhibited their wares. By the standards of the fully-fledged nineteenth century industrial exhibition, this was a comparatively small affair. But, rather than the somewhat earlier exhibitions at the Society of Arts (since 1908 the Royal Society of Arts), this exhibition established the form which subsequent industrial exhibitions were to take.

15 See Eugène Pierron, 'Les Expositions Universelles', in *Revue de l'Exposition Universelle* (eds F.G. Dumas and L. De Fourcaud), Paris 1889. Eugène Pierron (1848–98) assisted Contamin and Charton in the calculation of the stresses of the trusses in the Palais des Machines.

16 Adolphe Alphand studied civil engineering at the École Polytechnique and at the École des Ponts et Chausées. After directing work in ports, railways and land reclamation in Gascony, he was summoned to Paris by Haussmann in 1854 and spent the rest of his working life there. During the reign of Napoleon III, he was responsible for the administration of roads, tree-planting, sewerage, lighting and public works in general. Alphand created the Bois de Boulogne and the Bois de Vincennes. He played an important part in the siege of Paris during the Franco–Prussian War in the fields of munitions and fortifications. He was greatly involved with the exhibitions of 1867 and 1878 – for which latter he created the Parc de Trocadéro.

See *1889. La Tour Eiffel et l'Exposition Universelle*, Paris, 1989 (catalogue of the centenary exhibition at the Musée d'Orsay).

17 This exhibition was sited on the former gardens of the Royal Horticultural Society which were to the south of and adjacent to the Royal Albert Hall. The exhibition grounds and fountains were illuminated by some 9,700 electric lights; there were four generators. The exhibition galleries were lit by 430 electric arc lamps.

See Frank Cundall (ed.) *Reminiscences of the Colonial and Indian Exhibition*, London, 1886, pp.102-3.

18 The Eiffel Tower was the outcome of a collaboration between Eiffel, the Alsatian-born Maurice Koechlin (1856–1946), who was responsible for the initial sketch and the calculations and the architect Stephen Sauvestre, who brought a modest degree of refinement to the structure. Significantly, Sauvestre was never a student of the École des Beaux-Arts; this may explain the Eiffel Tower's generally coarser character – when compared with the exhibition work of Dutert and Formigé. It is possible that Henry-Russell Hitchcock, unaware of the full facts, relegated Dutert to the status of a lesser figure like Sauvestre when discussing the Palais des Machines.

The Musée d'Orsay centenary exhibition catalogue, *1889. La Tour Eiffel et l'Exposition Universelle*, includes a fairly detailed account of the history of the Eiffel Tower.

19 Edouard Lockroy was Minister of Commerce and Industry. On 3 April 1886, Lockroy published a bill to consti tute the forthcoming exhibition of 1889 as a government undertaking. He proposed that the system for financing the 1867 exhibition be reverted to – that is that the state be primarily responsible, but supported by a publicly accountable guarantee company. Thereby the evils of excessive private speculation would be avoided. See F.G. Dumas and L. De Fourcaud (eds) *Revue de l'Exposition de 1889*, Paris, 1889.

20 Leon Battista Alberti (1404–72) discusses *partitio* in *De Re Aedificatoria*, written in about 1450, which first appeared in printed form in 1485. The conception is associated with the placing of ornament on a building according to the proper division and subdivision of the parts of the structure. He demonstrated the application of the principle of *partitio* in Santa Maria Novella, Florence. Here, upon what was a medieval structure, Alberti imposed Renaissance order, by means of an ingenious system of applied classicizing elements. His marble marquetry, with its clearly defined linear divisions, demonstrates the power of simple geometry in the successful articulation of a façade. One could say no less of Dutert's façade on the Avenue de la Bourdonnais. See also my account 'Ornament and Form' in *The Routledge Companion to Contemporary Architecture*, London, 1993.

21 See Gisheler Hartung, *Eisenkonstruktion des 19 Jarhunderts*, Munich, 1983, p.38, fig. 15. Although this has a much smaller span than St Pancras (approximately 32 metres, as opposed to 74 metres) so similar is the form of the truss, that it is not inconceivable that Barlow and Ordish were influenced by it.

22 See Marie-Laure Crosnier Leconte, 'La Galerie des Machines' in *1889. La Tour Eiffel et l'Exposition Universelle*, Paris, 1989. To this I add that Schwedler was clearly toying with the idea of a hinged apex to the trusses of the retort shed of the Berliner Imperial-Continental-Gas-Association of 1863, although here the apex hinge was used in order to facilitate construction and not to compensate for expansion (see also note 21).

23 Eugène Pierron (1848–98) was trained at the École Centrale. Most of his career was spent in the service of the Ville de Paris, where he rose to the rank of Architect Inspector in Chief. He designed several Parisian schools. Pierron contributed to *Revue de l'Exposition Universelle de 1889*. See also *1889. La Tour Eiffel et l'Exposition Universelle*, Paris, 1989.

24 Jules-Jean Charton (d.1921). Like Pierron (note 23), Charton was trained at the École Centrale. He was employed by the railway Compagnie des Chemins de Fer du Midi. See *1889. La Tour Eiffel et l'Exposition Universelle*, Paris, 1989.

25 The antefix, in Classical (particularly Greek) architecture, is a small carved block – sometimes decorated with a motif like the anthemion – which was used to conceal the junctions of roof tiles. Leo von Klenze (1784–1864) in his competition design for the Glypothek, Munich, 1815, appears to have been one of the earliest neo-Classical architects to have revived the use of the antefix. Schinkel was also fond of it. Garnier, in the Paris Opéra, 1862–75, used antefixes – decorated with masks. Henri Labrouste, in his restoration drawings of the Temple at Paestum, of 1828, was liberal in his application of antefixes (see also note 26).

26 The drawings for the restoration of the Temple at Paestum, of 1828, by Henri Labrouste (the architect of the Bibliothèque Ste-Geneviève (1836–59) and the Bibliothèque Nationale (1855–75)) mark the beginning of the École des Beaux Arts tradition of creative restoration. Labrouste's rendered drawings, with their scientifically cast shadows, are typical of the genre of Beaux-Arts restoration drawings. Charles Garnier produced a fine restoration of the Temple of Jupiter at Egina in 1852–53. Victor Blavette, who aided Dutert during the building of the Palais des Machines, produced restoration drawings of the Temple of Demeter at Eleusis which won him a Première Medaille at the Salon of 1885 (see also note 8). See *Paris – Rome – Athènes. Le Voyage en Grèce des Architectes Français aux XIXe et XXe Siècles*, Paris, 1982.

27 The belief that Greek architecture was originally painted in bright colours – reds, greens, blues and yellows – had its origins in the eighteenth century. Stuart and Revett first published their discovery of fragments of pigment on ancient buildings in their *Antiquities of Athens*, London, 1762-1816. Labrouste, in his drawings of Paestum of 1828, applied discreet colouring to some of its mouldings. It was the German-born architect Jacques-Ignace Hittorff (1792–1867), however, who was the most vociferous champion of the cause of polychromy. His *Restitution du temple d'Empédocle à Sélinonte; ou l'architecture polychrome chez les Grecs*, Paris, 1851, contains magnificent chromolithographic plates which, whatever their historical accuracy, inspired the generation of architects which included Garnier and Dutert. Later architects, like Otto Wagner and Joseph Maria Olbrich, seem also to have drawn inspiration from Hittorff's ideas.

28 See *Joseph M. Olbrich, 1867–1908. Das Werk den Architekten*, Darmstadt, 1967 (catalogue of an exhibition at the Hessischen Landesmuseum).

Bibliography

Adge, Michel *Les Ouvrages d'Art du Canal du Midi*, Montpelier, 1983 (a published master's dissertation which establishes that a sophisticated tradition of civil engineering existed in France as early as the late seventeenth century).

Alphand, A. *Exposition Universelle de 1889 a Paris... Monographie*, Paris, 1892.

Anon *Engineering*, XLVII, 3 May, 1889 (an account of the buildings of the 1889 Exhibition). *The Architectural Record*, New York and Boston, January 1901. (This issue was devoted to the École des Beaux-Arts. See in particular John Mead Howells, 'From "Nouveau" to "Ancien" at the École des Beaux-Arts'.)

Barre, L.A. *Elements de Charpenterie Métallique*, Paris, 1870 (a standard work – the 1873 edition contains drawings of the roof structure of the Paris Universal Exhibition of 1867).*Black's Guide to Paris and the Exhibition of 1889*, Edinburgh, 1889.

Blavette, Victor Obituary of C.L.F. Dutert in *L'Architecte*, 15 June 1906.

Bloch, Jean-Jacques and **Delort, Marianne** *Quand Paris allait 'à l'expo'*, Paris, 1980 (includes details of the international Paris exhibitions 1855–1937).

Chadwick, George F. *The Works of Sir Joseph Paxton*, London, 1961.

Crosnier Leconte, Marie-Laure 'La Galerie des Machines' in *1889. La Tour Eiffel et l'Exposition Universelle*, Paris, 1989 (catalogue of the centenary exhibition held at the Musée d'Orsay, May–August 1989).

Drexler, A. (ed.) *The Architecture of the École des Beaux-Arts*, New York, 1977.

Durand, J.N.L. *Recueil et parallèle des édifices de tout genre, anciens et modernes*, Paris, 1801.

Durand, J.N.L. *Précis des Leçons d'Architecture*, Paris, 1802–9.

Dumas, F.G. and **De Fourcaud, L.** (eds) *Revue de l'Exposition Universelle de 1889* (two volumes), Paris, 1889. (Volume 1 contains Tancrède Martel's account 'Le Palais des Machines', pp.217–44. The high literary quality of this production is worth remarking upon.) *L'Exposition de Paris (1889)*, Paris, 1888–90 (a periodical published during the time of the exhibition and bound in two volumes). *Figaro Exposition 1889* (English edition), Paris and London, 1889.

Giedion, Siegfried *Space, Time and Architecture, the growth of a new tradition*, Harvard and London, 1941.

Glucq *L'Album de l'Exposition 1889*, Paris, 1889. *Les Grands Prix de Rome d'Architecture de 1850 à 1900. École Nationale des Beaux-Arts Cinquantaire*, Paris, n.d. (contains details of Dutert's winning Prix de Rome entry of 1869 – Palais d'un Ambassade française).

Hartung, Gisheler *Eisenkonstruktion des 19 Jahrhunderts. Mit einer Einführung von Professor Gunter Behnisch*, Munich, 1983 (this is probably the best recent account of the subject).

Hitchcock, Henry-Russell *Architecture: Nineteenth and Twentieth Centuries*, Harmondsworth, 1958.

Huysmans, Joris-Karl *Certains*, Paris, 1889 (a facsimile edition is still in print). *Jahrbuch des Deutschen Werkbundes 1914*, Jena, 1914 (includes photographs of contemporary German railway architecture which show some large steel trusses and suggest the influence of the Palais des Machines).

Lemoine, Bertrand *Gustave Eiffel*, Paris, 1984.

McGrath, Raymond and **Frost, A.C.** *Glass in Architecture and Decoration*, London, 1937.

Middleton, Robin (ed.) *The Beaux-Arts and nineteenth-century French architecture*, London, 1982.

Middleton, Robin and **Watkin, David** *Neoclassical and Nineteenth Century Architecture /2. The diffusion and development of Classicism and the Gothic Revival*, London, 1987 (first published in 1977). *Official Catalogue of the Paris Universal Exhibition, 1889*, London, 1889 (includes details of the British exhibits in the Palais des Machines). *Paris – Rome – Athènes. Le Voyage en Grèce des Architectes Français aux XIXe et XXe Siècles*, Paris, 1982 (catalogue of an exhibition which includes biographical details of the architect Victor Blavette who wrote the principal obituary of Dutert. This is the best source of information on the École des Beaux-Arts restorations of antiquity).

Pevsner, Nikolaus *Pioneers of Modern Design*, Harmondsworth, 1960 (first published as *Pioneers of the Modern Movement*, London, 1936).

Picard, Alfred *Exposition Universelle Internationale de 1889 à Paris. Rapport General*, Paris, 1891–92 (ten volumes).

Rousselet, Louis *L'Exposition universelle de 1889*, Paris, 1895.

Thorne, Thomas (ed.) *The Iron revolution. Architects, Engineers and Structural Innovation, 1780–1880. Essays to accompany an Exhibition at the RIBA Heinz Gallery June–July, 1990*, London, 1990 (contains an invaluable bibliography). *Twentieth Century Engineering*, New York, 1964 (published by the Museum of Modern Art, with an introductory essay by Arthur Drexler).

Vierendeel, A. *L'Architecture Métallique au XIXe Siècle à l'Exposition Universelle de 1889 à Paris*, Brussels, 1890.

Villari, Sergio *J.N.L. Durand (1760–1834). Art and Science of Architecture*, New York, 1990.

Viollet-le-Duc, E.E. (principal editor) *Encyclopédie d'Architecture. Revue Mensuelle*, Paris, 1872–77 (contains details of St Pancras, competition designs for the Paris Universal Exhibition buildings of 1878, Saulnier's Chocolat Menier factory etc.).

Viollet-le-Duc, E.E. *Entretiens sur l'Architecture* (two volumes and an atlas), Paris, 1863– (the atlas is dated 1864).

Viollet-le-Duc, E.E. *Discourse on Architecture* (trans. Benjamin Bucknall), London, 1877–82 (a facsimile of New York edition of 1889 was published in 1959).

Walmisley, Arthur T. *Iron Roofs. Examples of design. Description, illustrated with working drawings*, London, 1884 (second edition 1888) (contains details of the roofs of all the major British railway stations – including Lewis Casson's King's Cross (1851–52), Robert Hood's Victoria and Barlow and Ordish's St Pancras (1863–75)).

Weinreb and Breman Ltd *Catalogue 20. The use of Iron in construction and decoration. With a supplement of trade catalogues from foundries and ironmongers*, London, n.d. (1967) (a bookseller's catalogue with useful annotations).

Zeldin, Theodore *France, 1848–1945* (two volumes), Oxford, 1973.

Chronology

1845 Charles-Louis-Ferdinand Dutert is born in Douai (Nord).

1851 Bibliothèque Ste-Geneviève, Paris, designed by Pierre-François-Henri Labrouste (1801–75), which had begun in 1842, is completed. This was the first major architectural work in which an iron structure was frankly displayed.

1852–54 Paddington Station, London is built. Engineer: Isambard Kingdom Brunel (1806–59). Architects: Matthew Digby Wyatt (1820–77) and Owen Jones (1809–74). Maximum span: 102 feet (31.08 metres).

1855 Palais de l'Industrie, Exposition Universelle, Paris is built. Designer: Max Berthelin (1811–77). This was greatly influenced by Paxton's transept of the Crystal Palace, 1851.

1858 H.D. Maniton, Chief Engineer of the Compagnie du Nord, uses hinged bases for a 45 metre railway bridge at Saint-Denis on the Paris-Creil line.

1860–62 Victoria Station, London is built. Engineer: John Fowler (1817–98). Spans of each of the two train sheds: 130 feet (39.62 metres).

1863 Dutert joins the École des Beaux-Arts; he enters the atelier of Paul-René-Leon Ginain, the successor to Hippolyte Lebas (the teacher of Henri Labrouste).

1863– Publication of Viollet-le-Duc's *Entretiens sur l'Architecture* begins (it was completed in 1872). *Entretiens* contains a number of illustrations which suggest the possibility of a novel architecture employing iron structurally.

1868 St Pancras Station, London is built. Train shed designers: W.H. Barlow (1812–1902) and R.M. Ordish (c.1827–1886). Span: 243 feet (74 metres). Details published in *Encyclopédie d'Architecture*, volume 2, 1873.

1869 Dutert wins the Prix de Rome for the design of the residence of the French ambassador in an unspecified foreign capital. During his time in Rome he makes restoration drawings of the Forum.

1870–71 France is defeated in war with Prussia.

1875 Dutert wins a Gold Medal at the Salon for his Forum restoration drawings. He is also awarded the Prix Duc by the Académie des Beaux-Arts for his projected design for an Academy of Commerce. (Blavette, who wrote his obituary claimed that this was the first occasion on which Dutert asserted his individuality in a design.)

1875–77 Main station, Budapest, Hungary is built. Architect: G. Salard. Engineer: T. Seyrig. Gustave Eiffel collaborated in this project. It has a large curtain wall which may have inspired Dutert in his design for the Palais des Machines.

1878 Main exhibition building, Exposition Universelle, Paris is built. Architect: Léopold Amadée Hardy (1829–94). This was among the most innovative of nineteenth century glass-metal buildings. Eiffel had some influence upon the structure, although Duval was credited as engineer.

1879 'Au Bon Marché', 22 rue de Sèvres, Paris is built. Architect: Louis-Auguste Boileau (1812–96). Engineers: Armand Moissant and Gustave Eiffel. This was the earliest department store – iron and glass were liberally employed in its construction.

1881 Exposition Internationale de l'Electricité, Paris is held. This was the first major exhibition at which the potential applications of electricity were displayed.

1884 8 November, Jules Grévy (1807–91), President of France sets up a Consultative Commission to plan the Universal Exhibition of 1889. Days before this date, Dutert had submitted plans for exhibition buildings in the Invalides and on the Champ de Mars.

1885–87 Frankfurt-am-Main Station, Germany is built. Architect: G. Herrmann P. Eggert (1844–1920). Engineer: Wilhelm Schwedler (1823–94). Span of each adjoining train shed: 56 metres. This incorporated hinged trusses.

May 1886 Dutert wins competition for the design of buildings for the Exposition Universelle. Jean-Camille Formigé (1845–1926) and the partnership of Gustave Eiffel (1832–1923) and Stephen Sauvestre (born 1847) are the other winners.

24 March 1887 Contracts for the Palais des Machines are put out to tender.

10 June 1887 Contracts for the foundations are put out to tender.

5 May 1889 The Exposition Universelle opens.

31 October 1889 The exhibition closes with a total attendance of 28 million people.

1906 Dutert dies after a prolonged illness.

1909 The demolition of the Palais des Machines.